C O N T E X T S

Series Editor:

Steven Matthews

Oxford B⌇⌇⌇⌇⌇ ⌇⌇⌇⌇rsity, UK

Other titles in the series

Romantic Literature Jennifer Breen, University of North London, UK
Modernism Steven Matthews, Oxford Brookes University, UK
Renaissance Drama Andrew McRae, University of Exeter, UK
Renaissance Poetry James Loxley, University of Edinburgh, UK

VICTORIAN FICTION

GAIL MARSHALL

School of English, University of Leeds, UK

A member of the Hodder Headline Group
LONDON
Distributed in the United States of America by
Oxford University Press Inc., New York

First published in Great Britain in 2002 by
Arnold, a member of the Hodder Headline Group,
338 Euston Road, London NW1 3BH

http://www.arnoldpublishers.com

Distributed in the United States of America by
Oxford University Press Inc.,
198 Madison Avenue, New York, NY10016

British Library Cataloguing in Publication Data
A catalogue record for this book is available from the British Library

Library of Congress Cataloging-in-Publication Data
A catalog record for this book is available from the Library of Congress

ISBN 0 340 76328 0 (hb)
ISBN 0 340 76329 9 (pb)

1 2 3 4 5 6 7 8 9 10

Production Editor: Rada Radojicic
Production Controller: Martin Kerans
Cover Design: Terry Griffiths

Typeset in 10 on 12 pt Sabon by Phoenix Photosetting, Chatham, Kent
Printed and bound in Great Britain by MPG Books Ltd, Bodmin, Cornwall

What do you think about this book? Or any other Arnold title?
Please send your comments to feedback.arnold@hodder.co.uk

for Lily

Contents

Series editor's preface

The plural in the title of this series, *Contexts*, is intentional. Literature, while it emerges from, and responds to, historical, social and cultural moments, also to a large extent establishes its own contexts, through the particular inflection it puts upon its ostensible 'materials', themes, and preoccupations. Therefore, rather than offering a traditional 'major works/historical background' parallel discussion, each *Contexts* volume takes its instigation from the ways in which literary texts have defined their areas of reference, and in which they are in active dialogue with key cultural ideas and events of their time. What aspects of a period most concerned writers? What effect upon literary form have various social and cultural trends had? How have different texts responded to single historical events? How do different texts, ultimately, 'speak back' to their period?

Historical background is made readily available in each volume, but is always closely integrated within discussion of literary texts. As such, the narrative woven around each literary historical period in the individual volumes follows no uniform pattern, but reflects their particular author's sense of the ways in which the contexts of their period establish themselves – generically, thematically, or involving debates about language, gender, religion or social change, for example. While each volume provides detailed discussion of its period's most studied literary works, it also asks informed questions about the canon and periodization itself. Each volume also contains a timeline, full bibliography, and several contemporary literary, cultural, or historical documents which provide material for further reflection and discussion.

Steven Matthews

Acknowledgements

I am very grateful to those friends and colleagues, including Tracy Hargreaves, Francis O'Gorman, Juliet John, Jane Wood, Adrian Poole, Fiona Green, Elleke Boehmer, Inga-Stina Ewbank and Bridget Bennett, who have kept me in touch with work and the nineteenth century during the maternity leave and extended period of study leave in which this book was written. While away from my home university of Leeds, I have been indebted to Margaret Knight, the Harrow School librarian, for her efforts in searching through the school's reserve collections for me. I would also like to thank Steve Matthews for offering me the chance to work on this book, and for being a good friend and encouraging editor throughout.

The book has also incurred a number of debts which are more domestic than academic, more about contexts than texts. I owe enormous thanks to Petra Turner and Zoë Wilson for keeping Lily happy when I was writing; and to my parents and brother for their continued support. My greatest appreciation goes to Andy Todd, for reading *Bleak House* to me in traffic jams, for lending books, being sceptical, and sounding interested.

This book is dedicated, with much love, to Lily, whose own growing delight in books is part of the great joy she brings to every day.

Gail Marshall

Introduction

Novels and their readers

In writing about texts and their contexts, a number of questions are raised about precisely what is a text and what a context. In an age like the Victorian, when novels and novelists were frequently items of public debate, or themselves deliberately entered into the discussion of political and social matters, the lines begin to blur; the novel not only informs, but is context, part of the texture through which lives are lived and understood. That much, I think, will become clear in the book that follows, as we read of Charles Dickens's and Elizabeth Gaskell's interventions in the social questions of their day, or of the novelists of the 1890s who played a significant part in igniting the degenerationist panic which informed the *fin de siècle*. The precise nature of the relationship between novel and historical moment is, however, one which demands close attention, and it is with the nuances of that connection that we are concerned here, with the variety of ways in which the 1832 Reform Act is invoked as novelists recur to its seminal moment throughout the century; with the absence of significant reference to the Irish Famine in a century which was constantly aware of the rebellious island which refused to accept its almost colonial status, and which thus threatened to undercut the whole imperial project; and with the quiet omnipresence of the domestic setting, the background for many of fiction's most consequential encounters, but often actually at the heart of what is at stake in the novel.

As twenty-first-century readers, we have to be attentive to the quietness of a text on certain issues, perhaps concerning the family most of all. The Victorian family, and its 'values', are often casually invoked by conservative commentators and politicians keen to enrol them within their own contemporary vision, and in a sense the Victorian period itself allows that conscription by its own proclamations on the desirability of a certain configuration based upon the mother's presence within the family home, and the father's in the workplace. The most often invoked description of this structure is John Ruskin's account in 'Of Queens' Gardens' (1865):

> The man, in his rough work in open world, must encounter all peril and trial . . . But he guards the woman from all this; within his house, as ruled by her, unless she herself has sought it, need enter no danger, no temptation, no cause of error or offence. This is the true nature of home – it is the place of Peace . . . And wherever a true wife comes, this home is always round her.[1]

Yet, the briefest of comparisons between Ruskin and any Victorian novel will show us how far he is actually advocating the state he describes, rather than illustrating an existing state of affairs.

It is rather the case that children might be orphaned; that beyond the middle classes (who made up a far smaller proportion of the population than they do today), the home might be a site of poverty and suffering which the mother is powerless to avert; and that the mother herself might often be missing. The phenomenon of the absent mother is worth noting. The traumas of childbirth with neither anaesthetics nor antiseptic practices for most of the century were significant and highly dangerous, and often proved fatal. When coupled with the other health risks of the nineteenth century, it is little wonder that so many households were in fact presided over by maiden aunts, governesses, or housekeepers. The absence of the mother may indeed have been the only way of sustaining the desideratum aspired to by Ruskin, so difficult is it to conceive of any woman surrendering her being so entirely and unequivocally. This absence is variously recorded by novelists, from Dickens's traumatic description of Mrs Dombey's death in *Dombey and Son* (1846–48) to the simple absence of Dorothea and Celia Brooke's parents in *Middlemarch* (1871–72). However they are written, and however they signify within their own texts, those absences are the result of existing medical and social circumstances, and are thus indivisible from our awareness of the more public contexts of history.

In reading fiction alongside, or perhaps rather within, its historical moment, we inevitably gain some sense of how histories are written and constructed, of how certain narratives are privileged and selected as representative or significant, with others falling by the wayside as being of more limited contemporary concern. But we need also to be aware of the similar processes by which literary history, and indeed university and exam board syllabi, have pre-selected novels for our attention. The 'canon' of Victorian novels and novelists, growing bigger though it is, still represents only the tiniest fraction of the fiction that the Victorian period produced. And most of it falls within the category of expensive hardback fiction, which itself was only available to a small proportion of the literate Victorian population. Before going further we need to consider the publishing and reading contexts of the relatively small number of novels which we think of nowadays as Victorian fiction.[2]

Novels

In the Victorian period, novels were published in a variety of ways. Almost all of them would have first appeared in the form of a serial in a periodical publication, whether a daily or weekly newspaper, or one of the monthly periodicals. Much of the newspaper fiction never made it into hardback, and so is largely lost to us.[3] Most of the novels we read today would first have been seen in the pages of monthly publications, such as *Macmillan's Magazine*, which first published Charles Kingsley's *The Water Babies* (1862–63); the *Cornhill*, in which Trollope's *Framley Parsonage* appeared between January 1860 and April 1861 with illustrations by Millais; or the slightly more low-brow and popular *Temple Bar*, which was more heavily reliant on fiction than most of the monthlies, and included a quantity of sensation fiction by women writers, including Mary Braddon, Rhoda Broughton, and Mrs Henry Wood. Some sense of the publishing context of these novels may be gleaned if we look at the contents of a typical edition of the *Cornhill*, in which George Eliot's *Romola* appeared between July 1862 and August 1863, with illustrations by Frederic Leighton. The contents page for October 1862 reads thus:

> [George Eliot] 'Romola', chapters 15–20; [Edwin de Leon] 'How we broke the blockade' (of Confederate Ports); [George Henry Lewes] 'The effects of railways on health'; [Anne Ritchie] 'The Story of Elizabeth', part 2; Richard Doyle, 'The Smoking Room at the Club'; [M.A. Goldschmidt] 'A Norwegian musician'; [Theobald Matthew] 'Capture of the Delhi prizes'; [George Henry Lewes, George Hooper and J.F.W. Herschel] 'Our survey of literature and science'; [Anthony Trollope] 'The Small House at Allington', chapters 4–6.

(Names were not generally attributed to articles, but have been recovered by the editors of the *Wellesley Index of Victorian Periodicals*.) What is important here, then, is that most novels were not read in the isolation which usually accompanies our reading of fiction today. As well as a vast range of articles and learned reviews on contemporary matters, the novel would also be accompanied by a host of advertisements reminding the reader of the world out of which that novel was published. These publications were, however, at a cost of between 1 and 3 shillings, priced for a middle-class readership to buy. The newspaper fiction was more affordable, at around a penny a week, but still represented something of a luxury which, if bought, would usually be shared between neighbours.

During the century, novelists experimented with alternative publication methods, especially when their fiction looked set to exceed the bounds of usual practices. Eliot's *Middlemarch* was published in eight two-monthly parts in 1871–72 when it became clear that the novel would need to go beyond the more usual three-volume format. The format gave Eliot greater flexibility than the usual periodical publishing arrangement which she had found frustrating during the writing of *Romola*, and which had condemned Mrs Gaskell's *North and South* to an extremely hasty ending when it appeared in Dickens's weekly magazine *Household Words* between September 1854 and January 1855. The decision also proved lucrative for Eliot, as many more people bought the eight parts than might have been expected to part in one go with the 30–40 shillings which a novel usually cost.

The trend for part-publication had been begun by Dickens with *The Posthumous Papers of the Pickwick Club* which appeared in 20 monthly parts, between April 1836 and November 1837, finishing with a double issue. Dickens maintained this practice throughout his career, and it arguably contributed significantly to his success, and indeed to his formation of a national audience for fiction, as we will see below in Chapter 1. Dickens was well placed also in the mid-1830s to take advantage of the recent development of the railways which for the first time facilitated the swift transportation of text around the country, and enabled the simultaneous consumption of a novel throughout the land. As the century progressed the phenomenon of the best-seller became more familiar, and peaked in the 1890s with sales of Bram Stoker's *Dracula* (1897) and George du Maurier's *Trilby* (1894), which featured the villain Svengali. By then, marketing, distribution, and printing processes were in place to enable large print-runs and sales, but Dickens was the first fully to exploit the modern possibilities of the nineteenth century in selling his novels.

Readers

Only for the relatively wealthy were novels the objects of private consumption that they are for us today. Few except the most comfortably middle-class would have purchased the novels when they were issued in the three-volume format (which was dominant for most of the century) at the end of their serialized run. The average cost of a novel, like most prices in the nineteenth century, remained fairly constant at 31 shillings and sixpence, which easily exceeded the weekly wage both of labourers who might earn between 12 and 17 shillings and of most skilled craftsmen who might expect something between 28 and 35 shillings. Even on a low middle-class income of £160 per annum, the expenditure of 31 shillings on a book would have had to be a very careful decision.[4] It was far more usually the case that novels, and indeed newspapers, were borrowed and widely circulated, rather than individually owned. Some of these arrangements would have been made on a local basis, perhaps through the libraries of the working men's institutes which thrived in northern industrial cities in the mid- to late nineteenth century, and which were an invaluable first step into education for many.

The best-known of the borrowing institutions of the nineteenth century was Mudie's Select Library, begun in London in 1842 by Charles Edward Mudie.[5] Mudie's was a circulating library, from which its patrons might borrow one book at a time for a single fee of one guinea (that is, 21 shillings) per year. This was by far the cheapest rate of such an institution, and helped to ensure the success of the venture. Mudie swiftly expanded his premises in London, and branched out into the regions with bases in Birmingham and Manchester. He offered a postal service to subscribers, enabling even the most far-flung readers to stay in touch with recent publications, and also supplied texts to book clubs and provincial societies. Mudie swiftly became one of the most influential figures in the British literary world, controlling as he effectively did the fortunes of novelists. Careers were decided by Mudie's decision as to whether he chose to stock a novel or not, and the number of copies he chose to buy. His patronage was a difficult one to negotiate for publishers, who depended on his purchases, and his advertisements of new volumes, but who also found themselves under pressure to sell to him at heavily discounted rates or risk losing a sale altogether. Mudie could most effectively make or break an author, as George Eliot ruefully acknowledged when complaining to her publisher John Blackwood in 1859 about Mudie's omission of her *Scenes of Clerical Life* (1857) from his advertisements.

Mudie's ultimately proved to be a conservative hold on the literary world in more than one sense. His particular lending strategy meant that he was keen to see three-volume publishing practice continue, as he could effectively lend the novel out in three parts, thus keeping more customers supplied at greater profit than he could if each novel might only be lent out as a single entity. This was difficult enough, and often led to authors padding out novels with extraneous material in order to fill three volumes, or to publishers increasing margin or print size in order to take up more room. Mudie thus artificially manipulated, and probably held back, the evolution of the novel. His moral influence, was, however, perhaps even more invidious, and was more strongly felt as the century progressed, and as novelists began to experiment with the critiques of conventional practices, and particularly of generally accepted rules of sexual morality. For a parent, the great virtue of a Mudie's novel was that it could confidently be made available to any member of the household, having already gone through a form of censorship process. Thomas Hardy describes the influence of this process on the novel thus:

> the object of the magazine and circulating library is not upward advance but lateral advance; to suit themselves to what is called house-hold reading, which means, or is made to mean, the reading either of the majority in a household or of the household collectively. . . .
>
> As a consequence, the magazine in particular and the circulating library in general, do not foster the growth of the novel which reflects and reveals life. They directly tend to exterminate it by monopolising all literary space.[6]

Hardy goes on to bemoan the hypocrisy of a situation which censors the novelist who tried to represent issues and events which were the daily subject-matter of newspapers. Mudie was not alone in managing the reading-matter of the nation, but his was the strongest voice in the attempt to keep the novel free of moral controversy.

 Financial concerns were important in creating a class of novel readers, and in sub-dividing that class, but even more important, and not necessarily coterminous with that concern, was the ability to read. The Education Act of 1870 provided for the creation of elementary schools in all areas where church or other denominational schools did not meet the community's needs. These so-called board schools (because they were run by local boards) could make attendance compulsory, a principle which was extended to all schools in 1880. In 1891, these reforms were supplemented by elementary education being made free for all. Until this period, the ability to read was often a hit-and-miss affair for those whose parents could not afford schooling or the form of private tuition received by many middle-class children. It was not unusual for someone like Dickens's Joe Gargery in *Great Expectations* (1860–61) or Henry Mayhew's street-seller (see extract 1, p. 135) to pick up a smattering of letters, but such acquisition was not likely to turn them into novel readers. As we will see, however, the creation of a new class of readers following the 1870 Act and subsequent reforms generated a great deal of anxiety on the part of authors and cultural commentators, who saw the novelist's work suddenly taking on a whole new social responsibility.

Before the last quarter of the century, however, reading would have been for many a semi-communal affair, whether based in the home, a local place of entertainment, or one of the working men's institutes which regularly laid on readings and discussions of literature for their members. Just as books were not generally privately owned, neither were readings, which is something worth remembering as we ourselves read Victorian novels silently and alone. The rhetorical edge of Dickens is often clearly conceived with a live audience in mind, something Dickens himself took advantage of in his own reading tours. The performance of the text perhaps also sheds light on the popularity of melodramatic effect, not only in the sensation novels of the 1860s, but even in the generally more sober novels of George Eliot. Novels were a central part of the available entertainment for their readers for much of the nineteenth century, and it is perhaps only to be expected that the novel would necessarily borrow from other performance arts for its effects. Readers, therefore, are not just a passive market for fiction; rather, their conditions, expectations, and enthusiasms actively shape the novel.

The 'Victorian' period

The type of novel with which we are concerned here is, of course, the Victorian novel, a form popularly equated with the development of the realist text, though it had a plethora of forms besides, and with the consolidation of the newest of the literary art forms. But what precisely is 'Victorian'? When does the Victorian period begin and end, and how can the novel be read under that heading?

The dating of the Victorian period, or periods (early, mid- and late Victorian are all distinctions that are popularly and properly drawn) is primarily based around the reign of Victoria, from 1837 to 1901. But in this work I would like to propose a slightly longer period, beginning in 1830. This marked the beginning of the reign of William IV, a relatively short reign which served as a transition from the debaucheries of the royal family of the eighteenth century to the accession to the throne of the 18-year-old Victoria, who would establish the royal family rather than the exclusive person of the monarch as the leading image of the age. But 1830 is also significant in initiating a number of debates and narratives which came subsequently to mark the age with some of its most distinctive features. As we will see below (in Chapter 3), the late Victorians themselves saw 1830, and its specific transport and suffrage developments, as the beginning of their era. It essen-

tially saw the opening up of an era of democracy, not just in the limited parliamentary form, which itself was greatly remodelled as a series of Reform
Acts gradually enfranchised the bulk of the male population, but rather in
all aspects of work, education, and culture. Aspirations began to be
matched by mechanisms whereby literature, transport, employment, and
crucially literacy could be made more freely available as the century progressed. This rather comforting gloss is not meant to suggest that all was
well with every class. As Dickens, Mayhew and Gaskell show, the 'hungry
forties' and 1850s in particular saw terrible suffering, poverty, and death as
a result of some of the industrial developments and related demographic
shifts of the day. But, nonetheless, fiction could now make those ills known
to a much wider readership, and help to exorcize them.

Our period is characterized by a number of defining narratives which
appear and reappear in the book which follows, and which operate like the
'webs of affinity' of which Eliot writes in *Middlemarch*. Often apparently
independent of each other, as the narrative of the book will show they are in
fact rarely divorced, and more often are engaged in a deeply symbiotic
dynamic. Through the chronological progress of this book, we see those
threads emerge and re-emerge in different forms and combinations. It is
perhaps worth highlighting those narrative threads now in reminding ourselves of the primary determining conditions of the period.

Industry and technology

The Victorian period was one of massive technological innovation, in which
the scientist as well as the artist employed the imagination in creating or
discovering worlds previously unknown, and in forever changing the shape
and experience of the known world. The Industrial Revolution was already
under way as we enter the Victorian period, but it was during this time that
industrial technologies were most fully exploited, and large-scale factory
systems and the beginnings of a production-line style of manufacturing seen.
Goods from cloth to ready-made garments to industrial components could
all be produced more cheaply and efficiently than before, and to a higher
degree of accurate specification. The human cost of such developments was,
of course, immense, as John Ruskin and Charles Dickens both argued, most
notably in, respectively *Unto This Last* (1860) and *Hard Times* (1854), in
the latter of which Dickens sees whole communities systematically and
disastrously reduced to nothing more than their physical and economic
function. The human cost of industry, of the so-called Political Economy
which advocated a self-adjusting mechanism whereby gains and losses

would eventually reach some sort of equilibrium, was fiercely and emotively debated.

It is not, however, open to question that it was Britain's industrial and technological prowess which secured for the nation its international predominance in the mid-nineteenth century. On the fortunes of Britain's position in world markets rested its colonial exploits, as well as its diplomatic influence in world affairs. The ability to trade, to provide and indeed to create markets for goods which Britain could supply more cheaply and efficiently than any one else, cannot be overestimated. Colin Matthew claims that 'Victorian Britain [was] one of the most successful states in the history of the world',[7] and that this was so is largely dependent on the efforts of those inventors and innovators such as Isambard Kingdom Brunel, and the entrepreneurs who could exploit their work.

Such exploitation was only enabled by the parallel development of a transport revolution which meant that Britain could supply even the most distant market efficiently and relatively cheaply. A previous generation of engineers had concentrated on improving roads, and creating canals for the transportation of goods, but these methods of travel were limited by the speed of horses, and by the width of canals which often ran through developed areas, and which could handle only a finite amount of traffic. The first locomotive engine, George Stephenson's Rocket, ran on the Liverpool to Manchester railway which opened in 1830. Initially controversial, as it threatened livelihoods, and looked set to ruin the countryside, the development of a national railway network enabled the Victorians to enjoy a new mode of transport which revolutionized transport, communications, and even time itself. Until the growth of a national railway network, there was no need for a nationally agreed timetable. The Railway Act of 1844 made it compulsory for companies to offer travel for a penny a mile, thus making it available to the class of skilled workers, and enabling the workforce to become more fully mobile, and more able to respond to the demands of industry. After 1838, post was transported by rail, and this, along with the development of the penny post by Rowland Hill in 1840, and the system of telegraphs, whose wires usually lay alongside railway tracks, revolutionized people's ability to communicate. Developments in bridge and tunnel technology, backed up by the sheer number of labourers involved in blasting and clearing cuttings, meant that by 1847 most of the major cities of England were connected by rail.

These developments almost literally changed the shape of the Victorian world as it was experienced: just as the dimensions of the late twentieth century were altered by the innovations of the Internet, so were those of the nineteenth by steam and developments in iron production. But man's concept

of the universe, and his space and significance within it, were also challenged
in the nineteenth century by further scientific developments which, rather
than making new connections possible, were concerned to uncover relations,
to make links across time and across the spaces of the mind.

The work of the evolutionary scientists of the nineteenth century is
discussed in more detail below in Chapter 2, but I would just like to point
out here the ways in which they, and the practitioners of the new science of
psychology, like material scientists and inventors, similarly shifted the
paradigms of received experience. Long before the work of Charles Darwin
popularized the theory of evolution, or the evolutionary hypothesis, as it
was then known, geologists, such as Charles Lyell who published his
Principles of Geology between 1830 and 1833, and who provided part of
the intellectual context for Tennyson's *In Memoriam* (1850), had been
speculating about a world history which pre-dated that inscribed in the
Bible and whose mechanisms were in fact far more wonderful than the
miracle of the week of creation posited in Genesis. So, just as nineteenth-
century man seemed to be moving ever closer to making the world more
tractable and obedient to his wishes, evolutionary scientists were positing a
whole world-order pre-dating him and displacing him from the centre of
existence. He was to become just one in a series of stages of the development
of life on the planet, and one as likely to be superseded as any other archaic
and once-dominant form. The spectre of life without man is one that haunts
the narratives of progress which the Victorians espoused.

The science of psychology works similarly to complicate the equation of
hard work, virtue, and prosperity, as it added the dimension of the potential
unknowability and unpredictability of the mind and its workings to mid-
Victorian confidence in the exploits of man. Though working without the
concept of repression and of the precise notion of the unconscious later
popularized by Freud, Victorian scientists of the mind nevertheless significantly complicated received understandings of identity, memory, the
mind–body dyad, and the workings of dreams. Writers such as Wilkie
Collins, Sheridan Le Fanu, Charlotte Brontë, and George Eliot in particular
were ready to use the language and techniques of psychology in extending
fiction's capacity to reveal the contradictions or the full complexity of the
relations between personality and action, as well as to extend the
possibilities of fictional identity with such strange case-studies as the
characters of Le Fanu's Uncle Silas (in the novel of that name, published
1864), and George Eliot's hypochondriacal visionary Latimer (in 'The
Lifted Veil', written and first published in 1859).

As Jenny Bourne Taylor and Sally Shuttleworth point out in the introduction to their useful collection of Victorian psychological writings,

Embodied Selves (1998), by paying attention to the writings on the mind which were both widely available and widely read during the nineteenth century we can disabuse ourselves of some of the more lapidary notions we have about the Victorians: for instance, about their belief in 'a unified, stable ego' or that 'medical and psychiatric discourses represented a monolithic, almost conspiratorial desire to construct and police dominant notions of gender'.[8] But writings on evolution and psychology also re-shaped the mind-sets of their first readers, and profoundly influenced concepts of narrative and character for Victorian novelists.

Religion and belief

The development of an understanding of the mechanisms of evolution represented perhaps the greatest threat sustained by religious belief during the Victorian period. Its premises clearly invalidated the notion of God as omnipotent creator as propounded in Genesis and, despite Darwin's assertion in *The Origin of Species* that a belief in evolution was not incompatible with a sense of the wonder at the world (see extract 2, p. 137), his writings shook the possibilities of faith as it had previously been understood. In this it was joined by the importation of the Higher Criticism from Germany, which treated the Bible as a text just like any other, and which saw its structures and tropes within a literary-critical rather than a divinely-conceived context, thereby also striking at the roots of faith. It would, however, be wrong to regard these movements as having dealt a fatal blow to the possibilities of belief. Even during the 1890s, years characterized by doubt and despondency, and by the attempt to find more material explanations for the ills which seemed to be besetting Britain at the time, the majority of the country still maintained the customs of belief. This was at least in part because religion represented far more to the Victorians than it would to us today. Religious services provided a structure to the week, and an important social gathering-place. Sunday schools were often the principal source of primary education, and scriptural texts and hymns provided a common source of reading-matter and reference for the whole nation. It is impossible to overestimate the importance of religion for the Victorians, and the extent to which our society's relative lack of religious observance crucially sets us apart from the language, mind-set, and rhythms of Victorian life.

Victorian religion was far from being a monolithic form. The stereotype of the Victorian evangelical is well established, and was employed as a form of recognizable type by Dickens in several of his novels, by Charlotte Brontë in the figures of Mr Brocklehurst and St John Rivers (in *Jane Eyre* (1847)), and more probingly by George Eliot in the figure of Bulstrode in *Middlemarch*. Most striking, however, is the variety of forms of belief and practice of which we may read. In the work of Eliot alone we are introduced to the Methodism of Dinah Morris (in *Adam Bede* (1859)), to a carefully constructed range of opinions existing within the Anglican church in *Scenes of Clerical Life* (1857), and to the Dissenting Minister Rufus Lyon in *Felix Holt* (1866). We should remember, too, that the nineteenth century was a period which witnessed the integration of non-Anglican forms of faith into the establishment, into parliament, and into all levels of education. In 1829, Catholics were allowed to sit as Members of Parliament, and they were joined in 1858 by Jewish MPs. In 1871, fellowships in Oxford and Cambridge were opened up to non-Anglicans by the University Tests Act, which followed the abolition of religious tests for undergraduates at those universities in 1854 and 1856. This is not, of course, to suggest that Britain in the nineteenth century was not a place of some prejudice and occasionally strong distaste for those of non-Anglican faiths, but rather to emphasize that it was a country which was, however grudgingly, opening itself up to the full range of its constituencies as one of the conditions of its modernity.

An age of reform

This 'competition' from other faiths, notably from the dissenting congregations which defiantly opposed the practices of Anglicanism, was partly responsible for the reforms imposed upon the established Church in the 1830s. At that period, absentee rectors, who devolved responsibilities to underpaid and overworked curates, shared livings, and huge disparities in salaries and in diocesan fortunes were the norm. The Ecclesiastical Commission of 1835 proposed measures to address these conditions, which were enabled by Acts which restricted the holding of more than one post (the Pluralities Bill (1838)), and which fixed the salaries of some diocesan posts, abolished others, and facilitated the payment of clergy in under-represented areas with the surplus thus created.

These reforms were also prompted in part by the public outcry which followed the blocking in 1831 by the majority of the Bishops in the House of Lords of the second reading of the First Reform Bill, a measure designed significantly to extend the franchise. (When it was passed in 1832, the Great Reform Act almost doubled the size of the electorate from 409,000 to 814,000.[9]) Such intervention in the political process turned the spotlight on the Church and its own inequalities of practice. As we will see in Chapter 1 below, the 1830s were characterized very largely by the extent to which parliament was concerned to use its powers to intervene in matters such as public health and safety (in the Factory Acts of 1831 and 1833 which were principally concerned to limit the working hours of children); the relief of the poor (in the Poor Law Amendment Act of 1834); the abolition of slavery (achieved in 1834); and the reform of municipal councils (in 1835).

Much of the impetus to reform in the 1830s came about as a result of the massive changes in population distribution occasioned by the consolidation of the Industrial Revolution. London was the largest city in the world in the nineteenth century, but the rate of population growth was more important than sheer size alone. Greater London numbered 1.6 million people in 1821, 2.2 million in 1841, and 6.5 million by 1901. But Birmingham's population increased ten-fold to 760,000 between 1801 and 1901, and Bradford's growth was even more dramatic, increasing from 13,000 in 1801 to 280,000 in 1901.[10] Such rapid growth, which was also experienced, although at a slightly slower rate, in Bristol, Cardiff, Edinburgh, Liverpool, Manchester and Sheffield, generated problems of regulating the life and well-being of city-dwellers, of providing for the scale of their sanitary needs, and of providing safety-nets for those who fell casualties to the onslaught of the new industries.

Reform, in its many guises, was not primarily associated with a particular political party. Indeed, any one reform is likely to have been the result of fairly public manoeuvrings and carefully judged deals. Reform was most often a matter of expediency, to which all parties were subject. It is worth pointing out here that the main political parties of the nine-teenth century were not organized as are political parties nowadays, and were less easily associated with a particular range of issues and policies. Indeed, until mid-century there was considerable overlap between the par-ties' beliefs. It is also the case that the distinctions that did exist between the more conservative Tories and the Whigs, who had a more radical ele-ment, do not map easily onto the left–right distinctions parties were working with at the end of the twentieth century. As Clive Wilmer usefully points out, John Stuart Mill, a famous champion of democracy and women's rights, was also an advocate of utilitarianism and laissez-faire economics, and the High Tories William Wilberforce and Lord Shaftesbury were responsible respectively for the abolition of slavery and for the reforms of various Factory Acts. Their philanthropy emerged out of a Tory belief in the right to intervene, to govern actively, as part of an older tradition of landed influence.[11]

The motivations and mechanisms of reform shifted as the century pro-gressed, from the active intervention of politicians to less formal means of change, such as: the pressure of the specific interest groups who campaigned for the abolition of the Corn Laws and for married women's property rights; the lure of self-interest and a commitment to the desirability of a form of progress which began at home; and the self-regulating mechanisms of the free market. No matter how they were achieved, however, by the end of the century, the British population was healthier and better fed, better educated and housed than it was in 1800. It had moved from being, in Robin Gilmour's words, 'a predominantly rural and mercantile society, ruled by an aristocratic elite and a powerful Established church . . . to being a predominantly mercantile and industrial society, increasingly democratic and (within Christian bounds) religiously plural'.[12] Within that shift, the impulse of reform, often based on a recognition of how far national prosperity was founded upon a broad base of effort and industry, persisted as an effective democratization of access and opportunity.

Victorian women

The group whose lives were perhaps most radically transformed during the course of the nineteenth century was women, most notably middle-class women, it is true, but their efforts secured a number of reforms which benefited all. At the start of our period, all women were subject to the legal practice of 'coverture', which upon marriage entailed their absorption into the legal and financial standing of their husbands. A married woman had no rights over her own property, or her own person, and should the marriage end in separation she would have no right to her children. In 1854, Barbara Bodichon published a pamphlet 'A Brief Summary of the Most Important Laws Concerning Women; Together with a Few Observations Thereon'. It spelt out in great detail the legal vulnerability of women's position, and the essential fact that 'the good feeling of men [is] all that a woman can look to for simple justice'.[13] Bodichon was the illegitimate daughter of the radical MP Benjamin Smith, and wrote with some personal knowledge of the disabling nature of current legal practices. Bodichon was also one of the closest of George Eliot's female friends, and notably sympathized with the latter in the illegitimacy of her position as the unmarried partner of George Henry Lewes.

Bodichon's political activism was concentrated on the key reforms of the century, on women's education (she was one of the founders of Girton College), on the reform of property laws, and on women's suffrage. Advances were seen in all but the last of these areas as the century went on, but, despite the oratorical skills of women campaigners such as Bodichon, Millicent Fawcett, and Josephine Butler, of whom we will read more below, progress was slow and won with only the greatest effort. Women lacked direct representation in parliament, and could only work indirectly through a handful of male supporters, such as John Stuart Mill, who presented Bodichon's petition for women's suffrage to parliament in 1866. The pace of reform was also determined by the scale of the implications of change. Demands for legal, professional, and social equality challenged the fundamental grounds of distinct spheres, capacities, and interests upon which Victorian marriage, and indeed society, was based. The conservative rhetoric of separate spheres for men and women, no matter how little evidence for such absolute distinctions may be gleaned from our reading of fiction, was potently invoked as women's demands for reform were set up as challenging the stability of society, and the leadership of men.

Marriage and sexuality became key issues in the debate over women's rights and position, particularly in the 1880s and 1890s. Radicals like Eleanor Marx argued for the unhealthiness of women's chastity, and against the entrapment of marriage, and were backed up by Elizabeth Blackwell, one of the first women doctors, who argued for the strength of the sexual feeling which exists 'in so very large a proportion, in women's nature'.[14] Unlike earlier commentators, Blackwell also explicitly denies the idea that sexual activity, and specifically procreation, was incompatible with 'the utmost devotion to intellectual life, to lofty thought, to mental activities',[15] hence allowing for the possibility of women not being solely confined to the role of child-bearing. Thus, the monopoly of child-bearing and marriage in women's lives was effectively challenged, and other roles opened up.

It is, of course, ironic that the greatest argument against women being confined to a separate domestic sphere, and to a life solely consumed by children, was the figure of the woman who gave her name to the age we are looking at. As Barbara Bodichon wryly notes: 'The church and nearly all offices under government are closed to women. The post-office affords some little employment to them; but there is no important office which they can hold, with the single exception of that of sovereign.' Queen Victoria epitomized the multiple capabilities of women, as ruler, mother of nine children, and devoted wife and widow of Prince Albert. It was, as Dorothy Thompson argues in *Queen Victoria: Gender and Power* (1990), possibly her skilful negotiation of these various roles which led to her popularity and to the renewal of faith in a monarchy which had suffered greatly in the face of the public excesses of the eighteenth- and early nineteenth-century monarchs. She was also careful to deride the incipient women's movement, and to distance herself from claims for women's professional and public standing. In this, Victoria was simply the most public of a number of eminently successful women, such as the writers Margaret Oliphant and

Eliza Lynn Linton, who grounded their professional careers in impeccably responsible family reasons, and yet who categorically denied that those careers could be seen as evidence for women's professional aptitude. As we will see, the contradictoriness, and tortuousness, of such a stance is sadly typical of much thinking about women in the Victorian period.

Empire

Queen Victoria had a particular affection for the title of Empress of India which was bestowed upon her by the then Prime Minister Benjamin Disraeli in 1876, and afterwards was careful to sign herself Victoria R and I, Regina et Imperatrix. The adornment of the Empress title gave her precedence over mere monarchs, and its decorative function was mirrored in the colourful representation of the countries of the Empire in Victoria's Jubilee celebrations in 1887 and 1897, and in the artefacts of Empire, such as Indian shawls, and oriental china and tea, which embellished her subjects' homes. However, this function entirely misrepresents the importance of India, and of the rest of the Empire, to Victorian Britain. Economically, the Empire was crucial both as a market and as a source of raw materials such as ivory and cotton. Indeed, the primary mechanism of colonization was trade, practised first by private entrepreneurs, and then consolidated by government intervention. The East India Company governed India before the Indian Rising, or Mutiny as the Victorians knew it, of 1857, and maintained a monopoly on trade with China for much of the nineteenth century.

The Empire was constructed largely out of British needs, and had a profoundly symbiotic relationship with Britain. The activities of missionaries supported the incursions of traders, and provided an outlet for the profession of a faith which was being seriously challenged at home. Australia was the repository of convicts and 'fallen women' who could not be reclaimed within English society, and also provided fertile scope for those economic outcasts, such as Dickens's Mr Micawber (in *David Copperfield* (1849–50)) who found it difficult to prosper in the competitive arena of their homeland. It also provided further opportunities for the export of British successes, such as railways, and in terms of sheer geographical size helped Britain to compete on equal terms with its larger competitors, America and Russia.

Metaphorically, the Empire operated too as a means of articulating, of formulating, responses to aspects of the British experience which were unpalatable, but which, when confined within the metaphor of Empire, seemed to offer the possibility of resolution within existing parameters of experience and control. When William Booth published *In Darkest England* in 1890, he described the heathen state and suffering of much of England through the metaphor of darkness recently popularized by Henry Morton Stanley's tales of meeting David Livingstone in 'darkest Africa', and within that metaphor lies the form of solution to the problems he describes. If a controlling hand could be extended over the Empire, so it could too over the suffering and ignorant of Britain. The subsequent demise of the Empire, which was given considerable impetus by the Anglo-Boer War in South Africa (1899–1902), does nothing to invalidate the moral authority and hubristic world position which its Empire conferred on Britain for much of the Victorian period. In particular, it can be seen to inform Britain's response to Ireland, a colony at home for much of the nineteenth century. As we read of the means by which Britain extended its sway across India, Africa, Australia and Canada, we need also to be attentive to the ways in which that success is marked in fiction; rarely by explicit notice but rather by a more casual extension of consumerist rights and privileges.

These then are some of the narratives whose progress may be traced through the chronological chapters which follow, and which persist throughout the period, even when not explicitly noted. They persist sometimes as matters of topical news, sometimes as part of the grain of the everyday, almost too inherent to be noticed. This is perhaps where Victorian fiction enjoys an advantage over history, in its absorption in the minute particularities which make up representations of experience at different moments. There is, however, alongside this marking of time's passage, the suggestion that some things do not change, that emotional reality and its vocabulary persist across time, as might indeed be suggested by our own reading of Victorian fiction in the twenty-first century. In her introduction to *Felix Holt*, which carefully sets out the differences between the world of her characters in the early 1830s and the world of her first readers in 1860, George Eliot ends with a characteristic emphasis on the things that do not change, the emotional truths that persist despite developments in transport, housing, and voting patterns:

for there is much pain that is quite noiseless; and vibrations that make human agonies are often a mere whisper in the roar of hurrying existence. There are glances of hatred that stab and raise no cry of murder; robberies that leave man or woman for ever beggared of peace and joy, yet kept secret by the sufferer – committed to no sound except that of low moans in the night, seen in no writing except that made on the face by the slow months of suppressed anguish and early morning tears.[16]

Those sorrows provide part of the essential fabric of Eliot's belief in a fundamentally organic universe, and in a profoundly sympathetic if not empathetic aesthetic. But it cannot be denied that her characters' joys and sorrows are themselves grounded in a shifting historical reality, a fuller comprehension of which can only add to our engagement with Victorian fiction.

Notes

1 John Ruskin, 'Of Queens' Gardens', in *Sesame and Lilies* (London, 1911), pp. 87–143 (pp. 108–9).
2 Though the novel is the principal form of fiction with which this book is concerned, the short story will also be dealt with in the final chapter.
3 For more details of newspaper serializations, see Graham Law, *Serializing Fiction in the Victorian Press* (Basingstoke, 2000).
4 These figures are taken from Simon Eliot, 'Books and Their Readers', in Delia da Sousa Carrea, ed., *The Nineteenth-Century Novel: Realisms* (London, 2000), pp. 5–39 (p. 8).
5 The information on Mudie's library which follows is taken from Guinevere L. Griest, *Mudie's Circulating Library and the Victorian Novel* (Bloomington and London, 1970).
6 Thomas Hardy, 'Candour in Fiction', *New Review*, 2 (1890), 6–21 (p. 17).
7 Colin Matthew, 'Introduction: the United Kingdom and the Victorian Century, 1815–1901', in Matthew, ed., *The Nineteenth Century, 1815–1901* (Oxford, 2000), pp. 1–38 (p. 2).
8 Jenny Bourne Taylor and Sally Shuttleworth, eds, *Embodied Selves: An Anthology of Psychological Texts, 1830–1890* (Oxford, 1998), p. xiv.
9 Figures are taken from Anthony Wood, *Nineteenth-Century Britain, 1815–1914* (Harlow, 1982), p. 437.
10 *Ibid.*, p. 433.
11 See Clive Wilmer's introduction to John Ruskin, *Unto This Last, and Other Writings* (Harmondsworth, 1985), pp. 7–37 (p. 24).
12 Robin Gilmour, *The Victorian Period: The Intellectual and Cultural Context of English Literature, 1830–1890* (Harlow, 1993), p. 3.
13 Barbara Bodichon, 'A Brief Summary of the Most Important Laws Concerning Women; Together with a Few Observations Thereon', text supplied on 'Victorian Women Writers Project', www.indiana.edu/~letrs/vwwp.
14 Dr Elizabeth Blackwell, *The Human Element in Sex: Being a Medical Enquiry into the Relation of Sexual Physiology to Christian Morality* (London, 1884), p. 44. Marx's views can be found in her article on 'The Woman Question: From a Socialist Point of View', *Westminster Review*, n.s. 69 (1886), 207–22, which was jointly authored with her lover Edward Aveling.
15 Blackwell, *The Human Element in Sex*, p. 29.
16 George Eliot, *Felix Holt the Radical* (Harmondsworth, 1995), p. 10. This is the edition referred to throughout the book.

|1|

1830–1855
Living with the city

During this period, we witness the birth of the Victorian city and of the Victorian novel, and of a relationship between the two which was to prove of great importance and durability. Out of the city emerge crucial issues which find their most powerful expression in a new form of fiction and of fictional language which owe their birth in large part to the need to find ways of articulating new conditions. In some ways, novels and novelists fill the gaps of representation left by the disappointments of the electoral reform movement, giving voice to the otherwise unrepresented, and often calling into question the efficacy of more official political channels. Fiction is, during this period, a form of history, writing not only of the stories behind the statistics of reformers, but also of the conditions which bring about official silences and omissions. It is a form which demands to be read alongside the narratives of growing prosperity and national greatness with which the Victorians were preoccupied.

Early works of Charles Dickens:
the novelist in an age of reform

It is appropriate that the decade which witnessed the beginnings of the Victorian age also saw the emergence into print of the young Charles Dickens. For many, the writings of Dickens are synonymous with all that is deemed 'Victorian'. The endless adaptations to which his works have been subject, often even before the works themselves had been completed, have given Dickens's popularity a form of timeless appeal. For many later readers, this seems to consist of a fascination with recreating desirable 'certainties' which seem most fully embodied in the not too recent past. The allure of *A Christmas Carol* (1843) is a case in point. It has become a reassuringly constant part of the modern Christmases which the story itself is often held to have helped to invent.

However, to create a timeless Dickens, and indeed a commensurately non-specific 'Victorian age' out of the nostalgic desires and anxieties of more contemporary times is fundamentally to misread the achievements and popularity, and to overlook the radical newness, of the author. In the case of *A Christmas Carol*, it is to ignore the specific circumstances of suffering and social decay which provide the moral impetus behind Scrooge's reform. The years 1842–43 saw a depression in trade which led to strikes and the transportation of strikers from the North, and the second Chartist petition, which witnessed a series of social and political grievances. It was a time of unrest and of a lack of trust between employers and workers. That Scrooge's reform as both man and employer comes about in part through his greater knowledge of the plight of others gives a clue to Dickens's perception of the writer's ability to participate in a period of reform: ignorance in its many guises was for Dickens the primary social enemy. In reading Dickens, we need to take account of the specificities of his considerable political and sympathetic engagement with his own times, and also, most particularly, to take account of the extent to which Dickens might himself be said to have actively created both the age and the audience with which he now seems to be naturally synonymous.

In his biography of the writer, Peter Ackroyd argues that Dickens was the first novelist to take advantage of the possibility that a national audience for fiction might be created. Such a possibility of course demanded the presence of material factors such as cheap printing and paper-manufacturing processes, and the national distribution network made possible by the spread of the railways. But it also required that a novelist should somehow, as Ackroyd puts it, '[find] a voice which penetrated the hearts of the high as well as of the low', a voice which would be able to appeal to, and thus to create 'a national audience'.[1] Dickens was well placed to achieve this feat, as his own class-status was both ambiguous and typical of the new century in its fluidity. He was the son of John Dickens, a clerk, who was imprisoned for debt when Charles was 12 years old. This precipitated the break-up of his family at a time when Dickens had begun work in a blacking factory in London, many of the humiliating experiences of which are recreated in *David Copperfield*.

Through his journalism and fiction, Dickens went on to achieve a position of financial security sufficient for him to support his large family and to become an active philanthropist. However, far from securely inhabiting the middle-class world which his wealth brought him, he continued to enjoy the movement between and across classes which is demonstrated in his journalism, and in his earliest fictional works, *Sketches by Boz* (1836) and particularly *The Pickwick Papers* (1836–37). The writer Mary Russell Mitford wrote of *Pickwick* that:

> All the boys and girls talk his fun – the boys in the streets; and yet those who are of the highest taste like it the most. Sir Benjamin Brodie takes it to read in his carriage, between patient and patient; and Lord Denman studies *Pickwick* on the bench while the jury are deliberating.[2]

This may depend on the fact that:

> while 'Boz' brings before you with a graphic pen, the express image of the poorest and most ignorant orders, he never descends into vulgarity. The ordinary conversations of the loose and ribald multitude are faithfully reported, but by an adroit process of moral alchemy, all their offensive coarseness is imperceptibly extracted.[3]

In a tendency which would continue throughout his career, Dickens manages to exploit the impulses of both high and low culture in this work, to appeal to all kinds of audience in a demotic language and fiction which were, appropriately for their time, profoundly democratic and inherently new. For Andrew Sanders, Dickens embodies the 'essentially rootless dynamism' of the 1830s, and, in so doing, taps into the spirit of the age.[4]

For Thomas Carlyle, this was 'the Mechanical Age', 'the age of Machinery' which teaches that:

> our happiness depends entirely on external circumstances; nay, that the strength and dignity of the mind within us is itself the creature and consequence of these. Were the laws, the government in good order, all were well with us; the rest would care for itself! . . . It is no longer the moral, religious, spiritual condition of the people that is our concern, but their physical, practical, economic condition, as regulated by public laws.[5]

Carlyle's concerns about the 'moral, religious, spiritual' well-being of the people were well founded in an age which seemed increasingly, and necessarily, to be concerned with its economic and industrial strengths to the detriment of traditional ideas of community and family. But his is a characteristically idiosyncratic take on an age which many historians have subsequently regarded rather as an age of necessary and benevolent reform. Given the shift of a large portion of the population to the new, industrial cities, some new forms of regulation were clearly necessary to protect the people's well-being, and, less philanthropically, to head off the possibility that social unrest arising from poor living conditions might result in the kinds of revolutionary protest still besetting France.[6]

The reforming measures of the 1830s and 1840s embraced many aspects of contemporary life, some concerned with the welfare of the people, such as the six Factory Acts passed between 1831 and 1847, while others concerned the establishment and administration of Britain's burgeoning colonies (including Australia), the workings of the established church, and the formalization of the prison and court systems in Britain. An interesting factor of this age is the extent to which, as Andrew Sanders notes, extra-parliamentary pressure groups were able to exert significant pressure in effecting reforms such as the abolition of slavery (*The Spirit of the Age*, p. 54). The slave-trade had been banned for British subjects and ships since 1807, but it was not until 1833 that slavery in British colonies was abolished, largely due to the actions of William Wilberforce and an alliance of non-parliamentary Christian interests. Though the slavery question is not directly raised in Dickens's fiction, it is important to remember that the early Victorians lived in an age in which slavery had been an accepted practice. It is possible to argue that much of the rhetorical impetus and anger of Dickens's depictions of the suffering of unemancipated workers in his earlier novels, such as the 'hands' of *Hard Times*, and even the pickpockets of *Oliver Twist* (1837–39), derive from the congruence of his apprenticeship as a writer and the final years of slavery.[7]

Of more direct significance to readers of *Oliver Twist* is the Poor Law Amendment Act of 1834, a measure which is satirized in the early parts of the novel in the persons of the cruel beadle and the 'half blind and half childish'[8] magistrates who make up the governing board of the workhouse. The Act was brought in in the face of the increasing cost of welfare provision in the early nineteenth century. The Act tried to save money by outlawing 'outdoor relief', that is a system of allowances made in aid of wages in economically depressed times; and by making conditions in the workhouses to which paupers now had to apply for aid unpleasant enough to act as a deterrent to those seeking help. Within workhouses families were separated, and conditions maintained at such a level that not only the able-bodied but also the old and infirm suffered. As E.L. Woodward succinctly puts it, the poor law commissioners 'tried to make the status of able-bodied pauper less desirable than the position of the worst-paid labourer'.[9]

In 1837 a parliamentary Select Committee began to investigate the Act's workings and abuses, and, as Peter Ackroyd notes, it was also at this time that the Act's measures began to be felt in London (*Dickens*, p. 218). *Oliver Twist* was thus written, and first appeared (in magazine form, in *Bentley's Miscellany*), at a time when opposition to the new poor law was running high. The *Spectator*'s reviewer notes Boz's ability 'very skilfully' to '[avail] himself of any temporary interest to give piquancy to his pages', citing 'the popular clamour against the New Poor-law' as one such interest. Having quibbled with Dickens's interpretation of the law, he goes on to suggest that such opportunism may 'tell with many readers, but they must detract from the permanence of the writer who freely uses them'.[10] It was, however, precisely this ability to chime in with the feeling of the moment, to make use of 'the current phrase of the day' (Collins, *Critical Heritage*, p. 42), which was of the essence of Dickens's success at this period, and which arguably set him, and his fiction, apart from their predecessors.

His topicality, crucially enabled by serial publication, was not, however, simply a means of achieving popularity, but also secured for the novelist a polemic, campaigning voice, akin to that of the journalist (which of course Dickens also was), which had not been heard in the novel before, but which was to become a key-note of the rest of the century's fiction. Some of Dickens's most heart-felt concerns are sounded first in *Oliver Twist*: his pre-eminent concern for the integrity of the healthy family (which the Poor Law looked set to destroy) and its centrality within Victorian society; the implementation of the justice system; education, and the general welfare of the child; and the cause of the 'fallen woman', as exemplified in *Oliver Twist* by the loyal but morally irretrievable Nancy. Dickens's campaigning voice and methods would become more varied and sophisticated as his career progressed, but the simplicity of this novel's demand that the reader empathize with the lone figure of Oliver is highly effective, though perhaps marred for later readers by what might seem to be the author's social anxieties in giving his hero far better elocution than his social situation would allow. His genetic inheritance is already surfacing as we see him negotiate the slums of London in the company of Fagin's gang: a comforting prospect for the middle-class reader.

Coterminous with its reforming interests, *Oliver Twist* is also a novel about place, specifically about the place of home and characters' movements towards and away from that safe space. The stories of Rose Maylie, Nancy, Oliver and the lost boys of Fagin's gang are all dependent on their lack of a home, and on their desire to find and re-create a familial system around themselves. Indeed, much of the pathos of the novel is determined by Oliver's early loss of his mother, and the bass note which that lack, only too common for nineteenth-century children, sounds throughout the novel. This concern works in timely parallel with the novel's interest in the poor law reforms, at the heart of which was the question of where home was, and fundamentally, to where, geographically and institutionally speaking, a family might turn for relief. Traditionally a man's 'home' was deemed to be the parish of his birth, but the emergence of the new industrial cities, and the agricultural depressions of the early part of the century, meant that a demographic shift had begun which removed families from their birth-places in the search for work. The reforms to the poor law began to recognize that shift, and to institute a system of relief which was determined on a national basis rather than by the individual parish.

In *Oliver Twist*, we can see the beginning of the evolution of a national system out of a, literally, more parochial state of affairs. In the 1830s the parish was still a significant social component, and one which had its own structures and regimes. This is demonstrated in the early Dickens *Sketches* collectively entitled 'Seven Sketches from our Parish'. This fictionalized taxonomical survey scans the principal types of the parish, but begins with a mildly ironic definition of the powers of 'The Parish' which would be developed further in *Oliver Twist*. The plight of the indigent man is invoked:

> What can he do? To whom is he to apply for relief? To private charity? To benevolent individuals? Certainly not – there is his parish. The children have no protector – they are taken care of by the parish. The man first neglects, and afterwards cannot obtain work – he is relieved by the parish; and when distress and drunkenness have done their work upon him, he is maintained, a harmless babbling idiot, in the parish asylum.[11]

The prevalence of this social unit needs to be kept in mind when assessing this part of the century, for in many ways the 'nation' as we understand it now was only just beginning fully to emerge out of its component parts.

This may explain why, at this stage of his career, Dickens was so little concerned with the larger scale of national, and parliamentary, concerns, though we should note that he had also been left sceptical as to the efficacies of the political system by his early career as a parliamentary sketch writer, seeing the House of Parliament as an arena for the workings of private interests. Apart from a chapter of knock-about humour in *Pickwick*, and a parodic picture of an election in 'The Election for Beadle', one of the parish sketches, he makes scarcely any mention of one of the most far-reaching and contested reforms of the decade, the Great Reform Act of 1832.[12] The terms of the Act, which most notably extended the franchise to occupiers of buildings with a ratable value of £10, almost doubled the electorate but still only included one in seven adult males in the United Kingdom. No additional parliamentary seats were created, but some were redistributed away from the worst rotten boroughs to the new industrial towns of Manchester, Birmingham, Leeds, Bolton, Oldham, and Bradford. However, anomalies of

representation still persisted, and the South continued to be better represented than the North. In the wake of the passing of the Act, 'The Election
for Beadle' arguably relocates the national debates about voting abuses and
representation to their more appropriate site, the parish:

> The captain engaged two hackney-coaches and a cab for Bung's people –
> the cab for the drunken voters, and the two coaches for the old ladies,
> the greater portion of whom, owing to the captain's impetuosity, were
> driven up to the poll and home again, before they recovered from
> their flurry sufficiently to know, with any degree of clearness, what
> they had been doing. The opposite party wholly neglected these
> precautions, and the consequence was, that a great many ladies who
> were walking leisurely up to the church – for it was a very hot day –
> to vote for Spruggins, were artfully decoyed into the coaches, and
> voted for Bung.
>
> (pp. 40–1)

Interestingly too, of course, as this extract shows, these local elections
already gave votes to many people, notably women, for whom the
parliamentary franchise would long remain out of reach.

By far the most effective ameliorative measures in Dickens's early works
are those which operate locally, which are dependent on the concern of an
individual, and which are resolved through the means of the family unit. In
Nicholas Nickleby (1838–39) Dickens publicizes his concerns with the
'Yorkshire schools', more advanced versions of the baby farms of which he
wrote in *Oliver Twist*, and which seemed to perform a similarly grisly
function in, often permanently, removing inconvenient children from their
homes. Dotheboys Hall is the scene of appalling neglect, and its regime is
closely based by Dickens on the schools which he had visited with his
illustrator Hablot Browne. The novelist's exposure of the pupils' suffering
did what no political measure was currently concerned to do, in effecting
the closure of the worst of the schools in the face of public outrage.
Parliamentary Acts relating to children at this period were rather concerned
with the regulation of their working conditions, as the Factory Acts of 1833,
1842, and 1844, and Acts banning children working as chimney sweeps in
1834 and 1842, demonstrate. Basic educational provision was, however,
introduced through the 1833 Act, which among measures to cut down on
working hours also insisted that children aged 13 and under be at school for
not less than two hours a day.[13] At this time, schools came largely under the
control of religious organizations such as the English National Society and
the non-sectarian British and Foreign Society, with much reading being
taught also at Sunday Schools. After 1833, some factories also set up

schools, of often dubious quality, to conform with the Act. The principal mover of the 1833 Factory Act was Anthony Ashley Cooper, later the 7th Earl of Shaftesbury, who described his own first school as a 'Dotheboys Hall' (quoted in Woodward, *Age of Reform*, p. 145). Thus, although not himself a parliamentarian, there is evidence to suggest that Dickens helped politicians to find a language with which to recognize and to formulate their own responses to social distresses. Characteristically, this is achieved through the identificatory and empathetic act of immersion in a narrative, rather than the more aridly theoretical activities of argument and debate.

Within *Nicholas Nickleby* itself, Smike's escape from Dotheboys Hall and the demise of the school are just two of the acts of rescue performed by Nicholas Nickleby. Impelled by an innate sense of justice and social responsibility, which is based on his inherent sense of himself as the son of a gentleman, Nicholas also rescues Madeline Bray from marriage to the ancient and miserly Arthur Gride, protects the honour of his sister Kate from the onslaught of her aristocratic suitors, and rescues Newman Noggs from the service of his dissolute uncle Ralph. In Nicholas, moral virtue finally effects the cementing of ties of family: the discovery of a lost cousin in Smike, and the perpetuation of new generations in the marriages between Nicholas and Madeline, and Kate and Frank Cheeryble. We should also note that these marriages signal the happy coincidence of morality and money in the novel. Far from being its own reward, in this as in many later Victorian texts the hero's virtue is invalid or at least incomplete without the approbatory signal accorded by his achieving financial success, and securing his position within the middle class. By the end of the novel, that class status no longer rests solely on the implications of Nicholas's birth, but on his newly found ability to earn the accoutrements of his class.

Working alongside a reading which would stress the inescapable necessity of money in securing safety and stability is another highly distinctive aspect of the text which articulates for the first time the primacy accorded by Dickens to popular culture and its capacity to inculcate and indeed to embody a model of social harmony. Within the Crummles theatre troupe, Smike and Nicholas perceive an antidote to the tyrannical family model of the Squeers, and find themselves embraced within an organic community which can even find a productive place for Smike. As Mr Crummles explains:

Only let him be tolerably well up in the Apothecary in 'Romeo and Juliet' with the slightest possible dab of red on the tip of his nose, and he'd be certain of three rounds the moment he put his head out of the practicable door in the front grooves O.P.[14]

The Crummles family functions as a perhaps crudely systematic parallel to the Squeers grouping, but also provides our first glimpse of Dickens's belief in the moral efficacy of entertainment and communal laughter. In the creation of an audience, the theatre troupe and the novelist produce both an ameliorative cohesion (best effected through laughter) and the possibility of an empathetic response which might provide the foundation of a more morally effective and more content society. Taking full advantage of the technological developments and publication methods which meant that he could be a truly national novelist, Dickens found his moral function in the very proliferation of his art, both in exposing contemporary evils and in showing how his art could itself take on a moral capacity in bringing people together as an audience. Dickens's own philanthropic commitments to the causes of education, through reform of the Ragged schools, and fallen women, through the creation of homes for their reclamation, are well known. However, it does seem to be as a novelist that he felt he could best make his own contribution to this age of reform.

Dickens is not, then, simply the creator of Scrooge, of a timeless fairy tale, nor the sentimental novelist behind the death of *The Old Curiosity Shop*'s Little Nell (1840–41). Rather he was ineluctably involved in the questions of his time, both as interrogator and as himself an agent of change. The question of appropriate agencies of reform was one of which Dickens was unavoidably aware in this period. The revolutionary power of the 'mob', best demonstrated by activities in France and recalled later in *A Tale of Two Cities* (1859), was one towards which Dickens felt scepticism, fear, and a repulsion which was not without its fascinations, as is demonstrated in the description of the Gordon riots of 1780 in *Barnaby Rudge* (1841).

These rioters were protesting against the increasing civil rights being awarded to Catholics in Britain, but their actions took on a more immediate urgency and alarm for their first readers in the context lately created in Britain by the Chartists. The 'People's Charter' was published in May 1838 and was produced by the London Working Men's Association, an organization which was set up to 'draw into one bond of unity the intelligent and influential portion of the working classes in town and country, and to seek by every legal means to place all classes of society in possession of equal political and social rights' (quoted in Woodward, *Age of Reform*, p. 127). At its inception, therefore, the Chartist movement was not exclusively a working-class one. The Association, which had influence and membership beyond its London base, produced a Charter which was primarily ostensibly concerned with extending the political reforms which had begun in 1832. It:

sought to provide for the just representation of the people of Great
Britain in the Commons House of Parliament – embracing the
principles of Universal [male] Suffrage, No Property Qualification,
Annual Parliaments, Equal Representation, Payment of Members, and
Vote by [secret] Ballot.[15]

However, emerging as it did in a period when trade was depressed, and
when the introduction of machinery and the bite of the new Poor Law were
making living conditions increasingly intolerable for large numbers of
working-class families, the Charter was destined to carry a symbolic
resonance far beyond its stated remit. Arguably, it became the focus for
English revolutionary impulses in the period leading up to 1848, the year of
European revolutions.

Fiction and the years of revolution

Revolutions occurred in Sicily in January 1848, in Paris in February, when
King Louis Philippe was deposed, and in Germany and Italy in March.
That month also saw the fall of the Austrian Chancellor Metternich, who
was regarded by many as the architect of the 'Concert of Europe' (1815),
the peace which had been secured in Europe after the Napoleonic Wars.
More minor skirmishes also occurred in the cities of Venice, Berlin,
Prague, Budapest, and Milan. This was a period of political and national
(often nationalistic) unrest which, as Antony Harrison argues, was
dominated by 'the stand off between major powers, all eager to usurp
territory or protect what they already possessed'.[16] The revolutions were
not, however, simply concerned with international political matters of
leadership and governance. They also articulated grievances over issues of
welfare and social instability. Apparently more local in their effect, these
disputes were nonetheless experienced with an interesting degree of
synchronicity throughout Europe as the effects of industrialization were
made manifest in the form of increasing urbanization and an attendant
decline in living conditions. The latter was exacerbated by the crop failures
of the 'hungry forties', and further compounded by the potato blight
which hit the whole of Europe in 1846–47. Prices of food soared, as did
imports of staples, provoking many localized food riots. The food crisis
also contributed to unrest by impelling a further shift in the population
from agricultural to urban areas, creating a disaffected and hungry class
for whom the transition from a feudal to an industrial economy was
extremely painful.[17]

There was, however, no concomitant revolution in Britain in 1848, though the government feared a similar uprising. The Chartist movement had been a significant focus of local uprisings during the 1840s, and presented petitions in support of its Charter to parliament in 1839, 1842, and 1848. On each occasion the petition was rejected, but never more firmly than in 1848. Quite simply it seems that the conditions for revolution in Britain were not in place. Indeed, as a trading nation and an imperial power Britain was at this moment on the verge of a period of great prosperity. Apart from the appalling famine precipitated by the potato failure in Ireland in 1847, Britain did not experience food shortages at this time, in part because the Corn Laws, which had protected British agricultural interests and kept grain prices artificially high by restricting the import of foreign grain, had been repealed in 1846, thus making food significantly more affordable. This repeal was in part due to the work of the Anti-Corn Law League, a largely middle-class grouping which demonstrated how effective well-marshalled pressure might be in influencing government.[18] Lines of communication between rulers and the nation were then demonstrably open in Britain. This was evidenced also by the reforms designed to improve the lot of the proletariat (mentioned in the previous section) which were already in place.

England's more developed industrialized status meant that it had already come through the first throes of its transition to an urban economy, and, while not having solved all the attendant problems, there seems to have been at least an acceptance that the new and determining context of the nation was an industrial one. Accelerated industrialization also had the effect of moving the classes further apart from each other, and of cementing class distinctions. The British middle classes were benefiting from the enfranchisement secured by the 1832 Reform Act, which decisively separated their interests from those of the workers. Any revolt in 1848 would therefore have seen workers ranged not only against the government but also against a significant number of their fellow citizens. In proof of this, in addition to the 8,000 troops and 4,000 police called up to control the Chartist meeting on Kennington Common in April 1848, which preceded the presentation of a final petition to parliament, an estimated 85,000 special constables had been recruited, mostly from the middle classes, anxious to secure their homes and prosperity against the Chartists (Hoppen, *The Mid-Victorian Generation*, p. 130).

Rather than enveloping the country in revolution, then, the events of 1848 in Britain might rather be seen as confirming a new form of self-identification among workers whose traditional identities had been taken away with their agricultural occupations. The Chartists were instrumental in developing that working-class consciousness. In his chapter on 'Labour Movements' in *The Condition of the Working Class in England* (1845), Friedrich Engels writes of 'working men':

> a title of which they are proud, and which is the usual form of address in Chartist meetings, [that they] form a separate class, with separate interests and principles, with a separate way of looking at things in contrast with that of all property owners.[19]

Such an awareness of distinct class identities is developed in *The Communist Manifesto*, jointly authored by Engels and Karl Marx, which was first published in Germany in February 1848. The *Manifesto* expounds a theory of history which is based on constant struggle between classes. Analysing the 'modern bourgeois society that has sprouted from the ruins of feudal society', Marx and Engels find that it:

> has not done away with class antagonisms. It has but established new classes, new conditions of oppression, new forms of struggle in place of the old ones ... it has simplified the class antagonisms. Society as a whole is more and more splitting up into two great hostile camps, into two great classes directly facing each other: Bourgeoisie and Proletariat.[20]

Indeed the principle of antagonism is seen to define all social relations, setting even individuals against each other, in a context where money and business are deemed necessarily antagonistic to the claims of humanity. This state of conflict becomes in the fiction of the period a two-pronged dilemma demanding urgent attention and resolution: that is, how to find a means of reconciling the country's continuing economic development and success with recognition of the humanity of the operatives upon whom that success depended; and how to find a way to make the opposing classes of the bourgeoisie and proletariat speak and listen to each other.

These issues are played out clearly in Elizabeth Gaskell's *Mary Barton* (1848). The novel is set in Manchester in the late 1830s, a period when class configurations are being consolidated. The factory owner Carson had known poverty in his youth, and his wife was a former factory girl who was now awkwardly placed, 'without education enough to value the resources of wealth and leisure'[21] which her husband's wealth commanded. Her children are much more at ease in their newly moneyed world, despite its disfiguration by the schism between workers and employers. Described by Engels at this period as 'the second city of England, the first manufacturing city of the world', Manchester epitomized in its 'defiance of all considerations of cleanliness, ventilation, and health' (*The Condition of the*

Working Class, p. 92) the price paid by workers for the city's commercial well-being. Within the novel's analysis of working-class suffering and social schism, Gaskell shows how Chartism plays a crucial part in achieving a voice for the proletariat by giving it a focus for the development of a political consciousness:

> An idea was now springing up among the operatives, that originated with the Chartists, but which came at last to be cherished as a darling child by many and many a one . . . a petition was framed, and signed by many thousands in the bright spring days of 1839, imploring Parliament to hear witnesses who could testify to the unparalleled destitution of the manufacturing districts. Nottingham, Sheffield, Glasgow, Manchester, and many other towns, were busy appointing delegates to convey this petition, who might speak, not merely of what they had seen, and had heard but from what they had borne and suffered. Life-worn, gaunt, hunger-stamped men, were those delegates.
>
> (p. 127, ch. 8)

The rejection of that petition is brutally, viscerally, felt by Gaskell's hero, John Barton, but, as the novelist suggests, Chartism had given to working men their first political education, and most importantly a voice for the agonies of those whom Gaskell describes in her Preface as 'this dumb people'. Importantly, Gaskell also insists on using dialect for her Manchester speakers, another form of giving them a voice. In this crucial respect, Chartism also seems to have been significant in opening up public discourse to attractively vital new voices: as we will see, the fiction of the late 1840s is shot through with voices new both to fiction and to Victorian society.

Gaskell's 'Preface' identifies precisely the schism which Marx and Engels expose, and indeed argues that that perceptual gap is the key problem to be addressed, rather than the actual conditions faced by the workers, describing this feeling of alienation between the different classes of society as 'the most deplorable and enduring evil that arose out of the period of commercial depression' (ch. 8, p. 126). It is the feeling of having their wants ignored which she sees as likely to '[taint] what might be resignation to God's will, and turn it to revenge in too many of the poor uneducated factory-workers' ('Preface', p. 37). In response, Gaskell advocates that workers should be disabused of their 'miserable misapprehension' of neglect by 'private effort in the way of merciful deeds, or helpless love in the way of widow's mites' (p. 38). This conservative, meliorist attitude is, however, belied by the Preface's closing thought, written in October 1848, which reminds the reader of 'events which have so recently occurred among a similar class on the Continent' in such a way as to enjoin upon the reader a sense of the urgency of the British situation. Indeed, as the novel continues, with its grotesque catalogue of images of dying men lying half-naked on 'straw, so damp and mouldy no dog would have chosen it in preference to flags' (p. 100, ch. 6), of children (including John Barton's son) starving to death, and of desperate mothers, the cumulative weight of suffering depicted exceeds the limited scope of the Preface.

Gaskell's proposed solution lies outside the bounds of political economy, of parliamentary legislation, and indeed of Chartist revolution, rather being found within her faith as a Unitarian, and within the shared space occupied by the different generic strands of her novel. Unitarianism, a dissenting faith, was essentially interrogative in its relation to its historical moment, revolutionary even in its refusal to accept the status quo, and believing instead rather in 'a gradual progress to perfection, both in individuals and societies',[22] and thus enjoining upon the individual a personal responsibility to see justice done. It is, in the end, private acts of forgiveness which achieve long-lasting redemption in the novel. The novel's reconciliation between John and the elder Mr Carson is effected when the two men come together, not as operative and employer, but as fathers grieving for their dead sons, and for whom that experience of suffering exceeds their economic situation. Barton's repentance and Carson's forgiveness instate 'the spirit of Christ as the regulating law between both parties' (p. 460, ch. 44), thus denying class difference the determining significance and unambivalent meaning given it by such contemporary revolutionary thinkers as Marx and Engels, but doing nothing to diminish its significance as a new fictional as well as social force.

Raymond Williams suggests that the fiction of the 1840s, and especially that of 1848, is innovative primarily in that it 'admits class relations, including class conflict, as the conscious material of fiction',[23] and certainly, class differentiation plays a crucial part in each of the major novels to have come out of 1847–48. However, conflict is only one of the modes through which 'class' might be expressed. Georg Lukacs suggests that 1848 necessitated rather a new configuration of the classes, and the displacement of the 'ideologies of the bourgeoisie', which could no longer be regarded as 'the leading ideologies of a whole epoch, but simply class ideologies in a much narrower sense'.[24] The distinction is subtle but pivotal in understanding this period, in which not conflict but rather the bare possibility of disputing hierarchical certainties was crucial. Even the figure of God, as we have seen in Gaskell's dissenting text, and as some critics saw in *Jane Eyre*, might be drawn into this disputational moment.

Also at stake were the apparent certainties of inheritance and succession. The death of sons figures largely in the fiction of 1847–48.[25] The device signals in each fictional case a rupture with the past, and most significantly a disruption of the usual expectations of inheritance, in terms of both financial wealth and class position. The deaths are in effect revolutions in the novels in that they upset traditional expectations of primogeniture, and deny an organic, or more properly an evolutionary, progression. Often, as in *Mary Barton*, the death of the son will provide the fissure through which an act of class transgression can take place or may be confirmed. We might remember, also, that in *Jane Eyre*, Mr Rochester is the second son, whose position has necessitated his marrying Bertha Mason for her money; when his brother dies, Rochester's unexpected accession to his inheritance unleashes her colonial anger on his house.

The death of Paul Dombey is the central event of *Dombey and Son* (1846–48), and through it Dickens not only explores the dimensions of personal grief, but also gives his own version of the upheavals of bourgeois certainties in the years of revolution. It bristles with a variety of fictional forms which give voice to the panoply of lives and experiences of contemporary London. Set among the commercial houses and wharves of the capital rather than the industrial cities of the North, *Dombey and Son* is less concerned with the conflict of different classes than with the situations in which they are necessarily drawn together. For instance, Dombey fears the effects on his son and heir of his being nursed by the working-class Polly Toodle, and in a compensatory measure arranges for Polly's son to be educated, bringing that boy (named 'Biler' in Cockney homage to the wonders of the steam engine) into a position of confusion over his class identity which hastens his descent into crime.

Within the Dombey family, as well as within the city itself, Dickens exposes the potentially alienating effects of the new industries (and attendant commercial interests) identified by Marx and Engels. The principal representative of the capitalist world in this novel is the railway, first seen in the act of destroying as effectively as would an earthquake the home of Paul's nurse. The description is based on Dickens's witnessing of the building of Euston station between 1834 and 1838:

> Houses were knocked down; streets broken through and stopped; deep pits and trenches dug in the ground; enormous heaps of earth and clay thrown up; buildings that were undermined and shaking, propped by great beams of wood. Here, a chaos of carts, overthrown and jumbled together, lay topsy-turvy at the bottom of a steep unnatural hill.[26]

But out of 'the very core of all this dire disorder', 'the yet unfinished and unopened Railroad ... trailed smoothly away, upon its mighty course of civilisation and improvement'. Dickens is not being entirely ironic here. As Raymond Williams notes in his introduction to the novel, a new order is born out of the earthquake's chaos. The railway, like London itself, has become the heart of the nation: 'To and from the heart of this great change, all day and night throbbing currents rushed and returned incessantly like its life's blood' (p. 290, ch. 15). The railway is redeemed by this anthropomorphizing effect, and by its being imbued by Dickens with distinct moral qualities: it comes to seem entirely appropriate that the railway should be the means of killing Carker, the novel's villain, in a terrifying rush of wheels and steam.

At their worst, Dombey and the railways are forces of fatally depersonalizing commercial expediency, and are allied in the text with Major Bagstock's brutal colonialist attitudes, and with the impoverished underclass which was ever more present in a city which grew by 300,000 during the 1840s. These forces are jointly redeemed, however, by the story of Florence Dombey and Walter Gay, by their devotion to each other, which supersedes the class barriers and geographical obstacles which should have intervened, and by their affection for Mr Dombey and for the eccentrics who make up Walter's home. Out of the bruising city, Dickens brings humanity, and by replacing the commercial abstraction of 'Dombey and Son' with the lived family experience of Dombey and daughter, he demonstrates, perhaps rather optimistically, how the forces of the age may be domesticated and thus made productive, rather than annihilating.

The domestication of the dimension and discourse of class also informs one of the principal figures of the fiction of these years: the governess. The leading character in *Vanity Fair*, *Jane Eyre*, and *Agnes Grey* (all published in 1847), she not only demonstrates how intimately considerations of class necessarily penetrated into the home, but also reveals how definitions of gender depended upon appropriate class configurations. One of the most distressing documents of the agitation to improve factory conditions revealed how working-class women who went out to work effectively had their maternal rights denied in the most visceral way:

> M.H., aged twenty years, leaves a young child in the care of another, a little older, for hours together; leaves home soon after five, and returns at eight; during the day the milk runs from her breasts, until her clothes have been as wet as a sop.[27]

By contrast the middle-class woman, who probably did not work, adopted the governess to fill her role. Working as a governess was one of the few resources available to the impecunious lone middle-class woman who was reluctant to sacrifice her class status to her need for bread; indeed, her class status was her most eminent qualification for the role. The genteel governess protected young children from the attentions of a hired teacher, by masquerading as a substitute mother, in whose life the pecuniary question was deemed to take a peripheral role, lest the awkward contradictions she embodied, as a working middle-class woman and one who was also a childless mother-figure, became too pressing. Partly for this reason, many governesses ended their working lives facing destitution, and thus needed the help of the Governesses' Benevolent Institution, founded in 1841.

The annual report of the Institution for 1847 was reviewed by Elizabeth Rigby, later Lady Eastlake, alongside *Vanity Fair* and *Jane Eyre* in 1848, in an article which is primarily concerned with the stability of the author's own class. Though genuinely moved by the plight of retired governesses with no means of support, Rigby seems even more concerned by the growing numbers of governesses working in middle-class homes. Berating the mothers who thus abnegate their maternal duties, and consequently bring into question traditional definitions of womanhood, she also fears the consequences of recruiting governesses from a wider class than those distressed gentlewomen who had traditionally become governesses. As governessing became a career option for which 'Farmers and tradespeople' might educate their daughters:

> as a mode of advancing them a step in life, . . . a number of underbred young women have crept into the profession who have brought down the value of salaries and interfered with the rights of those whose birth and misfortune leave them no other refuge.[28]

Thus might other ranks infiltrate the homes of their superiors.

This is, of course, precisely what happens in *Vanity Fair*, where Becky Sharp uses her position to marry the younger son of the family in which she works, and from thence begins her dubious manoeuvrings within aristocratic and parliamentary society. Interestingly, however, it is Jane Eyre who attracts most of Rigby's wrath, and whom she finds an 'unregenerate and undisciplined spirit' who stands or falls by her own efforts: 'no one would think that she owed anything either to God above or to man below' (p. 173). Jane's own words bear witness to her pride and anger:

> Nobody knows how many rebellions besides political rebellions ferment in the masses of life which people earth. Women are supposed to be very calm generally: but women feel just as men feel; they need exercise for their faculties, and a field for their efforts as much as their brothers do; they suffer from too rigid a restraint, too absolute a stagnation, precisely as men would suffer; and it is narrow-minded in

their more privileged fellow-creatures to say that they ought to confine themselves to making puddings and knitting stockings, to playing on the piano and embroidering bags. It is thoughtless to condemn them, or laugh at them, if they seek to do more than custom has pronounced necessary for their sex.

(p. 141, ch. 12)

When read in the context of the rebellions of 1848, the discontented, dependent but genteel governess elides with the mass of rebellious workers, shocking contemporary reviewers such as Rigby who found in Jane's voice an echo of the troubles of 1848:

We do not hesitate to say that the tone of the mind and thought which has overthrown authority and violated every code human and divine abroad, and fostered Chartism and rebellion at home, is the same which has also written Jane Eyre.

To Rigby, the novel is 'pre-eminently an anti-Christian composition' in its 'murmuring against the comforts of the rich and against the privations of the poor', and it thus set itself against God's will, in asserting the 'rights of man' (Rigby, 'Vanity Fair, Jane Eyre', p. 174).

As the extract above shows, *Jane Eyre*'s impact is all the greater for being written in the first person. The effrontery of this voice clearly aggravates Jane's offence in Rigby's eyes, and indeed the form of the novel is part of the condition of its success and of its relationship with its times. The very fact of Jane's voice (and its as yet unconfirmed female authorship), like the newly public voices of the Chartists, was in itself an achievement in an age in which women were more usually concerned with private, domestic spaces than the public articulation of their discontents and desires. Indeed, this is a period in which the female novelist begins to come to the fore, despite the suspicion with which her role was often treated. In *The Daughters of England, Their Position in Society, Character and Responsibilities* (1842), Sarah Stickney Ellis had claimed of the female ambition to write that it was an ambition 'more productive of folly, and of disappointment, perhaps, than all the rest'.[29] Charlotte Brontë had received her own personal advice on becoming a writer from Robert Southey, to whom she wrote in 1836 of her proposed career as a poet. He replied:

Literature cannot be the business of a woman's life: & it ought not to be. The more she is engaged in her proper duties, the less leisure she will have for it even as an accomplishment & a recreation. To those duties you have not yet been called, & when you are you will be less eager for celebrity.[30]

Southey went on to advise her to write poetry for its own sake, and not for fame. Brontë's spirited reply defends her interest in writing, and her nicely judged sense of sarcasm sends up that sense of opposition between the female writer and the more proper woman which informs Southey's letter:

> I find enough to occupy my thoughts all day long, and my head and hands too without having a moment's time for one dream of the imagination. In the evenings, I confess, I do think, but I never trouble any one else with my thoughts. I carefully avoid any appearance of pre-occupation, and eccentricity, which might lead those I live amongst to suspect the nature of my pursuits.
>
> (Charlotte Brontë to Robert Southey, 16 March 1837, *The Letters of Charlotte Brontë*, p. 169)

By 1848, however, a context had been created which could accommodate an 'eccentricity' of voice. No novel demonstrates this better than *Wuthering Heights*. Though imbued with a contemporary notion of class differentiation which meticulously informs the distinctions between Wuthering Heights and Thrushcross Grange, *Wuthering Heights* articulates as its most compelling concern the passionate and definingly personal voices of Catherine Earnshaw and Heathcliff, which seem to emerge not from society but from the nature with which they are associated.[31] Prompted by the articulation of difference which the recognition of distinct classes necessarily entails, voices are sounded in the novels of 1847–48, from the dialect speakers of *Mary Barton* to the pagan anger or Irish hunger of Heathcliff, which were previously unheard in mainstream fiction.

Most significant is the way in which these voices operate within the texts. Raymond Williams argues of *Wuthering Heights* that its competing narrative voices do not require a final resolution, or act of singular identification on the part of the reader, but rather rest complete in their lambently antagonistic status. As he puts it, they make for a 'very complex seeing' ('Forms of Fiction', p. 284), what perhaps would be described by Mikhail Bakhtin as 'dialogism'.[32] A not dissimilar perception is voiced by Rigby in her review of *Vanity Fair*, in which she finds that 'the personages are too like our every-day selves and neighbours to draw any distinct moral from' ('Vanity Fair, Jane Eyre', p. 156): that is, they speak with competing and ultimately irresolvable voices. Things in *Vanity Fair* are indeterminate as real life is, a perception Rigby finds distressing in a novel in which the 'sense of dead truthfulness weighs down our hearts' (p. 156). Perhaps, out of this period, then, comes not a political revolution, but the possibility of a newly responsive, and politically responsible, form of fiction.

Counting the cost of political economy

In 1851, at the suggestion of Prince Albert, London mounted in the 'Crystal Palace' in Hyde Park 'The Great Exhibition of the Industry of All Nations', a showcase for arts and artefacts from around the world, and especially for the industrial achievements of the host country. In its dazzling spectacle of consumer goods, it provided confirmation of Britain's place at the forefront of world manufacturing. In the same year, the decennial Census showed that an unprecedented 43 per cent of the population was working in the manufacturing, mining, and building industries; that the population of the rural counties was dropping; and that people were continuing to move into cities. As Martin Daunton writes: 'For the first time in the history of the world, more than half of an entire national population was living in towns.'[33] Far from being a cause of economic and civic concern, however, this trend now seemed to herald still greater heights of industrial achievement. Quite simply, the Census and Exhibition of 1851 confirmed Britain as a dominant world power, and the Exhibition demonstrated the grounds and causes of this dominance. It enrolled the colonial nations within a display of patronage, and invoked them both as sources of raw materials and as markets for finished goods; it invited the working classes to special 'Shilling Days', where they were admitted at one fifth of the usual price, and were reported to be docile, well-behaved, and admiring of the displays, as well as being conveniently kept out of the way of the middle and upper classes;[34] and it advertised the power of the worship of commodities, of consumer display, and spectacle which foregrounded the actual economic terms of Britain's success in the nineteenth century. Though not itself a market, rather a gorgeous window-display, the Exhibition worked to excite the consuming instinct within its visitors, and thus to implicate and instruct them in their places in the delicate balance of supply and demand which governed nineteenth-century economics, the management of which was at the root of Britain's pre-eminence in the middle of the nineteenth century.

The Exhibition also notably divorced artefacts from the means and spaces of their production. In 1852, Queen Victoria would visit the Black Country, and record in her journal:

> It is like another world. In the midst of so much wealth, there seems to be nothing but ruin. As far as the eye can reach, one sees nothing

but chimneys, flaming furnesses, many deserted but not pulled down, with wretched cottages around them. . . . Add to this a thick & black atmosphere . . . and you have but a faint impression of the life . . . which a 3rd of a million of my poor subjects are forced to lead.

> (quoted in Matthew, 'Introduction: the United Kingdom and the Victorian Century, 1815–1901', *The Nineteenth Century*, p. 4)

No such discomfiting impressions were allowed in Hyde Park. But for John Ruskin, as for Marx before him, that very disjunction between labourer and finished goods, the masking of the conditions endured by those responsible for the glories of the Exhibition, was symptomatic of an age in which the demands of industry were making men into soulless tools. In 'The Nature of Gothic', the central chapter in Ruskin's architectural appreciation *The Stones of Venice* (1851 and 1853), he writes of how the precision engineering of the machine age demanded a division of labour which was also a division of the man:

> Divided into segments of men – broken into small fragments and crumbs of life; so that all the little piece of intelligence that is left in a man is not enough to make a pin, or a nail, but exhausts itself in making the point of a pin or the head of a nail.[35]

The demand for perfection needs to be sacrificed in order that 'that imperfection [which] is in some sort essential to all that we know of life' (p. 92) be allowed to flourish.

The ethos of 'The Nature of Gothic' is entirely opposed to the celebration that was the Great Exhibition, and may have been partly inspired by that event. On 1 May, Effie Ruskin went off alone to the opening of the Exhibition, while in his diary John wrote, proclaiming his antipathy to the Exhibition in every word:

> Morning. All London is astir, and some part of all the world. I am sitting in my quiet room, hearing the birds sing, and about to enter on the true beginning of the second part of my Venetian work. May God help me to finish it to His glory, and man's good.[36]

But Ruskin's real target was the notion of political economy, 'the art or practical science of managing the resources of a nation so as to increase its material prosperity' (OED) which underlay the principles, even the possibility, of a Great Exhibition. Developed first by Adam Smith in his *The Wealth of Nations* (1776), the theory is based on a belief in the ultimate motivation of self-interest, and the importance of increasing productivity, wherever and however possible. It divorced morality from the work-place, and regarded as necessarily doomed any attempt by government to interfere with the natural laws of economics, even when those laws included the inevitability of some part of the population being condemned to poverty.[37] Such views were, of course, anathema to Ruskin, and sit uncomfortably alongside the glossy spectacle of the Great Exhibition.

Also countering the confidence, even the hubris, of the Great Exhibition, were the challenges to religious faith and practice experienced at this time. These were various, ranging from a general unease with the Evangelical doctrines of hell and everlasting punishment, through to the schisms of the on-going Oxford Movement, which sought to find an authority in the Anglican church which many believed had been lost, and which had resulted in the rise of dissenting congregations. Many members of the Oxford Movement eventually turned to Catholicism. The German Higher Criticism, such as David Friedrich Strauss's *Das Leben Jesu*,[38] read the Bible as a historical text, subject to the same temporal determining factors as any other. And the challenge of science, whose geological developments cited evidence of gradual transformations of species in opposition to the divinely purposive Genesis narrative, was gathering speed. The ensuing fragility of some people's faith perhaps explains the heightened anti-Catholicism in evidence in England in 1850–51, following the restoration of the Roman Catholic hierarchy in 1850; but also led to the first Secular Society in London in 1851. The regular census of that year was accompanied by a religious census which showed that approximately five million people out of a total population in England and Wales of around eighteen million had not gone to a church on the Sunday being investigated by the census. In theological and practical terms, religious belief and practice were under threat.[39]

From the perspective of a largely secular society it is hard, perhaps even impossible, truly to appreciate the traumatic effect of these attacks on the possibilities of faith. The material universe, and men's lives within it, were no longer held to operate as proof of God's divine presence, and so faith had to be reconstituted, as 'a matter of inner conviction and the will to believe'.[40] Such is Tennyson's final persuasion in *In Memoriam* (1850), but it is a conclusion won only with difficulty, after the poet has faced the possibility of the complete dissolution of identity following his loss of faith:

> Behold, we know not anything;
> I can but trust that good shall fall
> At last – far off – at last, to all,
> And every winter change to spring.

So runs my dream; but what am I?
An infant crying in the night;
An infant crying for the light,
And with no language but a cry.

(Section 54)

In 'Dover Beach', which was probably written in the year of the Great Exhibition, Matthew Arnold also invokes a state of darkness, as he hears the 'melancholy, long withdrawing roar' of the 'sea of faith' and turns for succour instead to the promise of human relationship:

Ah, love, let us be true
To one another! for the world, which seems
To lie before us like a land of dreams,
So various, so beautiful, so new,
Hath really neither love, nor joy, nor light,
Nor certitude, nor peace, nor help for pain;
And we are here as on a darkling plain
Swept with confused alarms of struggle and flight,
Where ignorant armies clash by night.

In fiction, the figure of the clergyman provided the focus for such intensely personally felt challenges to individual spirituality, and indeed to the possibility of individuality as it had previously been conceived (that is, as deriving from the presumption that man was made in the likeness of God, and was specifically distinct from the animal world). Elizabeth Gaskell's Mr Hale in *North and South* (1854–55) is an Anglican clergyman who, though in no doubt as to religion, has to leave his church, and jeopardize his social standing, because of his inability to reaffirm the Thirty-Nine Articles which provide the basis of faith for the practising clergyman. Dickens's novels of this time contain Evangelicals who are cruel, hypocritical, and distinctly un-Christian. Following in the line of *Jane Eyre*'s Mr Brocklehurst (rather than her St John Rivers), Dickens's Murdstone in *David Copperfield*, though not a clergyman, is rendered cruel by the prospect of his own salvation, and damning to the young David who, not yet saved, is necessarily in a state of perdition. Though, as Robin Gilmour points out, Evangelicals were responsible for many of the century's great moral campaigns, including those against slavery and child labour, which emanated from their belief in the possibility of conversion through preaching and persuasion, by the 1850s those efforts were being regarded as sanctimonious and interfering, for instance in their insistence on a strict observance of the Sabbath: in 1855 their anti-Sunday trading stance provoked riots.[41]

What seems worse, for Dickens, is the way in which the professed faith
and works of ministers such as Mr Chadband (in *Bleak House*) not only
mask grasping materialism (as in his collecting money from poor children),
but actually blind him and his followers to pressing need at home, concentrating as they are on self-aggrandizing projects for the relief of the inhabitants of Borrioboola-Gha. Mrs Jellyby's gargantuan letter-writing efforts on
behalf of that benighted African country leave her own family in squalid
chaos, but also mean that she is wilfully ignorant of the needs of Jo, the
crossing-sweeper:

> he is not one of Mrs Jellyby's lambs, being wholly unconnected with
> Borrioboola-Gha; he is not softened by distance and unfamiliarity;
> he is not a genuine foreign-grown savage; he is the ordinary home-
> made article. Dirty, ugly, disagreeable to all the senses, in body a
> common creature of the common streets, only in soul a heathen.
> Homely filth begrimes him ... native ignorance, the growth of
> English soil and climate, sinks his immortal nature lower than the
> beasts that perish.[42]

Illiterate and wasted, Jo epitomizes the neglect experienced by those who
fell outside the sphere of productivity of industrial Britain. Similar stories fill
the pages of Henry Mayhew's *London Labour and the London Poor*
(1849–50), the title of which sets out the terms on which contemporary
society was divided. (See extract 1, p. 135.) Jo has his 'revenge', however, in
spreading the disease which infests his life through 'every order of society,
up to the proudest of the proud, and to the highest of the high' (p. 710,
ch. 46). Contagion, one of Dickens's greatest fears, operates as a reproach
against a society whose institutions, including that of organized religion,
necessarily impinge upon, but do nothing to nurture, the individuals who
make up that society. The legal world similarly presses upon Richard
Carstone in the interminable case of Jarndyce versus Jarndyce, ceasing only
when the plaintiffs run out of money to feed the legal machine:

> To see everything going on so smoothly, and to think of the roughness
> of the suitors' lives and deaths: to see all that full dress and ceremony,
> and to think of the waste, and want, and beggared misery it repre-
> sented ... was at first incredible.
>
> (p. 396, ch. 24)

The vulnerability of the individual to the institution is best demonstrated
by Dickens's *Hard Times*. The novel was inspired by an actual strike in
Preston, but moves beyond its industrial remit to consider also how
education, as another form of state institution or apparatus, and the

philosophy of utilitarianism, which underlies the science of political economy, kill off individuality in the creation of a uniformity of mind and response in the work-force of aptly named 'hands'.[43] Dickens shows education being enlisted in the services of utilitarianism (ironically, given that philosophy's belief in laissez-faire), to create a populace which knows only enough to know its place:

> To render education productive of all the utility that may be derived from it, the poor should, in addition to the elementary instruction now communicated to them, be made acquainted with the duties enjoined by religion and morality; and with the circumstances which occasion that gradation of ranks and inequality of fortunes which are of the essence of society.[44]

The system's greatest success is Bitzer who excels in his education at Mr M'Choakumchild's fact-based academy, and goes on to police Coketown from his surveillance point in the bank. Its greatest casualty is Stephen Blackpool, who dares to put his integrity before both the self-interest which is utilitarianism's foundation and the collective, bullying imperative of his union.[45] As a result, Blackpool is ostracized by all.

In 'On Strike', Dickens writes 'political economy is a mere skeleton unless it has a little human covering and filling out, a little human bloom upon it, and a little human warmth in it' (p. 465). For want of that little humanity, Stephen Blackpool dies a martyr, and the workers and manufacturers in Preston remain distrustful of each other. Some humanity, however, is to be found in the wonders of Sleary's circus which, like the theatre of *Nicholas Nickleby*, provides a respite from the 'melancholy madness' (*Hard Times*, p. 22, ch. 5) of money-getting. Located upon 'the neutral ground upon the outskirts of the town' (p. 14, ch. 3), the circus is in every way surplus to the rigid economy of Coketown, and as such is typical of the overwhelming concern of novelists, indeed of literature, at this period, with what exceeds the remit and calculations of political economy. Nonetheless, in that attention to excess, to the economically unproductive, the all-pervasive influence and shaping powers of 'economy' are to be felt.

In *David Copperfield*, the disposal of unproductive characters is instructive. The notoriously uneconomically minded Mr Micawber and his large family are packed off at the end of the novel to Australia. The early 1850s was the peak period for emigration there, providing:

> the greatest possible advantage to the empire in general, as affording a field of enterprise to more ardent spirits of the mother country, who, in the present peaceful times, cannot find a suitable career at home;

and also as creating and increasing thriving communities in that part of the world with which our manufacturers carry on a large and lucrative trade.[46]

Between 1852 and 1855, Ford Madox Brown worked on his painting 'The Last of England', which was inspired by the departure for Australia of his friend and fellow artist Thomas Woolner and his wife. Finding public and critics indifferent to his art, Woolner sought advancement overseas (but before the painting was completed was back in England again, disappointed in his travels),[47] and thus became part of the movement to encourage the middle classes to move to underpopulated parts of the Empire. A Family Loan Colonisation Society was founded to encourage women and children, 'God's police', as the founder of the Society, Caroline Chisholm described them (Hyam, *Britain's Imperial Century*, p. 43), to travel out. However, it is evident that Dickens uses the resource of emigration to rid England of troublesome spirits. As Mrs Micawber puts it, 'Mr Micawber is going to a distant country, expressly in order that he may be fully understood and appreciated for the first time' (p. 743, ch. 57). Australia enables the prosperous ending for the Micawbers which the reader might wish for, but which the economic conditions of contemporary England would not permit.

Australia also provides a resting-place for another kind of surplus, for Little Em'ly and for Martha, the fallen women whose sexuality is surplus to the increasingly ideologically crucial entity of the family. The line between prostitute and seduced girl, between voluntary emigration and transportation (still practised to parts of Australia until 1868), is blurred in a shared destination, which is also envisaged for the prostitute Esther in *Mary Barton*, and for Hetty Sorrel in George Eliot's *Adam Bede* (1859). The official reason for Hetty's transportation is infanticide, but clearly the domestic and social chaos caused by her desire for the squire's grandson renders her removal from England desirable. In literature and painting, female sexuality was emerging as a force troubling to the prosperity of the new Britain.

In the early 1850s paintings of the Pre-Raphaelite Brotherhood, a revolutionary group of artists who appropriately enough chose to constitute themselves as a group in 1848, female sexuality is represented as dangerous primarily to the women themselves. Rossetti had yet to paint his gorgeously vibrant 'stunners', and the Lady of Shallot (painted by Holman Hunt 1850, Elizabeth Siddal 1853, Millais 1854), Mariana (Millais 1851), and Ophelia (Millais and Hughes, both 1852) are rather wasted and doomed by the bondage which is their desire. These women are admonitory, rather than celebratory, and operate in a context in which the blight of sexuality was made highly visible in the figure of the fallen woman. It was during these years that Effie Ruskin, wife of John, met, modelled for, and fell in love with Millais, whom she married, after the annulment of her marriage to Ruskin on the grounds of non-consummation, in 1855. The fallen woman was also a cause for political concern: in 1850 the government had set up a Royal Commission on divorce, which resulted in the 1857 Divorce Act, a measure which inscribed the possibility of female adultery into the legislature. It was deemed sufficiently dangerous that women could be divorced on grounds of adultery alone, whereas men had to aggravate that offence by combining it with incest, bigamy, rape, sodomy, bestiality, cruelty, or desertion ('without reasonable excuse, for Two years or upwards').[48]

By contrast with the Pre-Raphaelite brotherhood, novelists are rather concerned to try to save their fallen women. Though they might die, it is suggested that death can itself be a redemption. *Bleak House*'s Lady Dedlock exemplifies this, as her death heightens our sympathy with her plight, with her efforts to rebuild her reputation in a subsequent marriage, and with her suffering under Tulkinghorn's prosecution. She has also, of course, been partially redeemed by the late recognition of her motherhood, a force which also comes to ameliorate the position of Gaskell's *Ruth* (1853), a seamstress seduced and abandoned by the upper-class Bellingham. In one of the most controversial novels of the decade, she goes on to bear his child and, after having been rescued by a mild nonconformist minister and his sister, goes on to live a life of moral purity and service. Though some of Gaskell's neighbours in Manchester burnt the book, her heroine was received on the whole with sympathy and understanding, perhaps because throughout Ruth remains curiously unsensual, untouched by her fall, and also because she dies at the end of the novel from typhus contracted through nursing the man who was her seducer.

In the novel's terms, her death is the confirmation of Ruth's redemption, curiously perhaps given the extent to which Gaskell downplays the sin committed, but the ending still jars with the modern reader as it did with Elizabeth Barrett Browning and with Charlotte Brontë.[49] For other contemporaries, however, it was fully in line with the view that Gaskell had done a service to the cause of 'penitentiaries, and nurses' institutions, and sisterhoods, and deaconesses' institutes' (*North British Review*, quoted in Helsinger *et al.*, *The Woman Question*, p. 117) for the reclamation of the fallen. Clearly, saving does not necessarily entail survival, nor, as Dickens demonstrates in his 1853 letter 'An Appeal to Fallen Women', full social inclusion. Writing of Angela Burdett Coutts's scheme to help rescue the fallen, Dickens writes:

And because it is not the lady's wish that these young women should
be shut out from the world after they have repented and learned to do
their duty there . . . they will be supplied with every means, when some
time shall have elapsed and their conduct shall have fully proved their
earnestness and reformation, to go abroad, where in a distant country
they may become the faithful wives of honest men and die in peace.[50]

Like Micawber, they may be virtuous, but England can have no place for
them. Curiously the fallen woman and the redeemed prostitute share the
same fate of displacement, for both are fundamentally disruptive of
morality, and also of economics. The fallen wife disrupted certainties of
inheritance and succession through her adultery, whereas the saved
prostitute had lost her economic function. Previously an intrinsic part of an
urban landscape, where late marriages were increasingly the norm as
couples waited to be able to afford to marry into a state of comfort, the
saved prostitute had relinquished her place within the political economy,
and thus was ideally removed from the country, lest her redemption raise
more disturbing questions about social morality, as Bernard Shaw's Mrs
Warren was to do in the 1890s.[51]

In *North and South*, however, Mrs Gaskell shows how female sexuality
may be reclaimed in a tale which is both morally and economically
exemplary. In Margaret Hale's famous public intervention in the strike in
Milton Northern, she seeks by virtue of her womanly status to mediate
between Mr Thornton and the anger of his striking workers. However, once
she goes public with her femininity, it is transmuted under 'a thousand
angry eyes'[52] into a sexuality which is both vulnerable and beyond
Margaret's own control. She realizes the extent of this vulnerability only
later as she experiences Mr Thornton's subsequent proposal as offensive to
her 'maiden pride' (p. 247, ch. 23). The strike triggers the emergence of a
sexuality which is troubling to Margaret, and which informs a series of
incidents which are misleadingly read through the prism of this awakened
force. Innocent throughout, except for a white lie told to protect her
brother, Margaret nonetheless experienced the sexuality foisted upon her by
others as a degradation. It is only finally redeemed and made safe by her
marriage to Thornton, an act in which, under the terms of mid-century
marriage, her legal, economic, and moral being are surrendered to him.

This marriage is also notable in being economically exemplary.
Thornton's business had been failing, and can be saved only by the gift to him
of Margaret's legacy from her godfather, Mr Bell. Previously converted by
Margaret into the kind of manufacturer approved by Ruskin in *Unto This
Last*, who considers not 'how to produce what he sells, in the purest and

cheapest forms, but how to make the various employments involved in the production, or transference of it, most beneficial to the men employed' (Wilmer, *Ruskin*, p. 178), Thornton now faces the poverty which Ruskin envisaged might come to one who would not compromise his principles in the interests of profit. Morality begets failure, but Thornton is saved by Margaret's love, and by their marriage can narrow the gap between the working environment and the home, engendering a productive and nurturing organicism beneath the shelter of his paternalism. All this is made possible by the incorporation of Margaret into an appropriate economic situation.

The relationship between women and economics is one of complexity and elisions. Ideally non-workers, non-producers except within the home, women were the still centre around which nation and economic prosperity were ideally configured. In 1854, Coventry Patmore published the first parts of his *The Angel in the House*, a celebration of the selfless, 'simply, subtly sweet' wife, installed on 'the throne/Of her affecting majesty' in the home. But in a later, less blissful, addition to the poem, published in 1879, the wife is likened to a foreign land, in which:

> The most for leave to trade apply,
>   For once, at Empire's seat, her heart,
> Then get what knowledge ear and eye
>   Glean chancewise in the life-long mart.

Women and emotions are thus installed in a life-long economic as well as domestic set of transactions. In her marriage Margaret Hale enters into a new economic status, that of consumer and housekeeper, the practitioner of that domestic economy which Gaskell gently satirizes and celebrates in *Cranford* (1851). Thus, morally secure, Margaret is also made secure in taking up her own role within Gaskell's idealized industrial economy. At best, morality should infuse the economic and industrial sphere, as it does that of the home and family. However, the dicta of political economy had sundered the two, and rendered the survival of the fittest a potent concept long before Herbert Spencer gave a name to it in his *Principles of Biology* in 1863. As the teachings of religion were called into question, and its denominations were themselves competing to survive, the metaphors and practices of economy assumed the space vacated by the monoliths of organized worship.

Notes

1 Peter Ackroyd, *Dickens* (London, 1990), p. 193.
2 Mary Russell Mitford, from a letter, 30 June 1837, quoted in Philip Collins, ed., *Charles Dickens: The Critical Heritage* (London, 1971), p. 36.

3 'Some Thoughts on Arch-Waggery, and in especial, on the Genius of "Boz"',
  Court Magazine (1837); *Critical Heritage*, pp. 33–5 (p. 35).

4 Andrew Sanders, *Dickens and the Spirit of the Age* (Oxford, 1999), p. 43. *The
  Pickwick Papers* has most readily been seen as an example of Dickens's early
  humour, and as a work which negotiated the transition between the picaresque
  tradition of the eighteenth-century novel and the 'realism' of the nineteenth.
  However in reading *Pickwick* it is also important to remember this comment by
  Thackeray:

  > I am sure that a man who, a hundred years hence, should sit down to write
  > the history of our time, would do wrong to put that great contemporary
  > history of *Pickwick* aside as a frivolous work. It contains true character
  > under false names; and . . . gives us a better idea of the state and ways of
  > the people than one could gather from any more pompous or authentic
  > histories.
  >
  > (W.M. Thackeray, in *The Paris Sketch Book* (1840), quoted in Sanders,
  > p. 38.)

5 Thomas Carlyle, 'Signs of the Times' (1829), in *Critical and Miscellaneous
  Essays*, Vol. II (4 vols, London, 1857), 98–118 (p. 106).

6 Just a year after Carlyle wrote, the French people rose again, and deposed King
  Charles X.

7 That the appeal to slavery might still operate as an effective political tool is
  demonstrated as late as 1869 in John Stuart Mill's *The Subjection of Women*,
  where he draws on the example of the slaves of America to help him to describe
  the life of unenfranchised British women. In *Jane Eyre*, too, Charlotte Brontë
  invokes the image of the 'rebel slave' in invoking the young Jane's situation (*Jane
  Eyre* (Harmondsworth, 1985), p. 44, ch. 2.

8 Charles Dickens, *Oliver Twist* (Harmondsworth, 1994), p. 25, ch. 3.

9 E.L. Woodward, *The Age of Reform, 1815–1870* (Oxford, 1938),
  p. 434. Woodward continues, however, that, if the commissioners 'did not
  always succeed, the reason lay more in the grim condition of the worst-paid
  labourers than in the compassion of the central or local authorities'
  (pp. 434–5).

10 Unsigned review of *Oliver Twist*, *Spectator* (November, 1838); quoted in *Critical
   Heritage*, pp. 42–3 (p. 43).

11 Charles Dickens, 'Seven Sketches from our Parish', in *Sketches by Boz*
   (Harmondsworth, 1995), pp. 17–66 (p. 17).

12 In fact this Act only receives its most significant fictional treatment much later, in
   George Eliot's *Felix Holt* (1866) and *Middlemarch* (1871–72), novels in which
   Eliot is concerned with the second Reform Act of 1867, and with looking back
   to the beginnings of the parliamentary reform movement in 1832.

13 Other provisions of this bill were that children under 9 years old could not work
   in textile factories, and those under 13 could only work up to 48 hours a week.
   Those under 18 could work up to 69 hours per week, those hours being between
   5.30 am and 8.30 pm.

14 Charles Dickens, *Nicholas Nickleby* (Harmondsworth, 1986), p. 356, ch. 22.

15 From the 'People's Charter' (1838), quoted in Edward Royle, *Chartism* (Harlow,
   1980), p. 88.

16 Antony H. Harrison, '1848', in Herbert Tucker, ed., *A Companion to Victorian
   Literature and Culture* (Oxford, 1999), pp. 19–34 (p. 20).

17 For useful accounts of the 1848 revolutions see Peter Jones, *The 1848
   Revolutions* (Harlow, 1981); and Charles Breunig, *The Age of Revolution and
   Reaction, 1789–1850* (New York, 1977).

18 Historians disagree over the extent of the League's responsibility for the reform of the Corn Laws. For opposing views see K. Theodore Hoppen, *The Mid-Victorian Generation, 1846–1886* (Oxford, 1998), pp. 11, 128; and Woodward, pp. 113–16.

19 Friedrich Engels, *The Condition of the Working Class in England* (Harmondsworth, 1987), p. 246. The first English translation, by Helen Macfarlane, appeared in a Chartist newspaper, *The Red Republican,* in 1850.

20 Karl Marx and Friedrich Engels, *The Communist Manifesto* (Oxford, 1998), p. 3.

21 Elizabeth Gaskell, *Mary Barton* (Harmondsworth, 1985), p. 254, ch. 18.

22 Jenny Uglow, *Elizabeth Gaskell: A Habit of Stories* (London, 1993), p. 6.

23 Raymond Williams, 'Forms of Fiction in 1848', in *1848: the Sociology of Literature,* ed. by Francis Barker *et al.* (University of Essex, 1978), pp. 277–90 (p. 280).

24 Georg Lukacs, *The Historical Novel,* trans. by Hannah and Stanley Mitchell (London, 1962), p. 174.

25 The sons in question are Edgar Linton and Hindley Earnshaw in *Wuthering Heights* (1847); George Osborne in *Vanity Fair* (1847–48); Paul Dombey; Mr Rochester's elder brother in *Jane Eyre*; and the sons of John Barton and Mr Carson in *Mary Barton.*

26 Charles Dickens, *Dombey and Son* (Harmondsworth, 1985), p. 120, ch. 6.

27 1844 House of Commons speech by Lord Ashley, later Earl of Shaftesbury, quoted in Elizabeth K. Helsinger, Robin Lauterbach Sheets, William Veeder, eds, *The Woman Question: Society and Literature in Britain and America, 1837–1883, Vol. 2: Social Issues* (Chicago, 1983), pp. 121–4 (p. 122).

28 Elizabeth Rigby [later Elizabeth Eastlake], 'Vanity Fair, Jane Eyre, Governesses' Benevolent Institution Report for 1847', *Quarterly Review,* 84 (1848), 153–85 (p. 179).

29 Sarah Stickney Ellis, *The Daughters of England, Their Position in Society, Character and Responsibilities* (London, 1842), p. 240. These views did not stop Ellis herself writing 11 novels between 1836 and 1881.

30 Letter from Robert Southey to Charlotte Brontë, 12 March 1837; in *The Letters of Charlotte Brontë, Volume 1, 1829–1847* (Oxford, 1995), pp. 166–7.

31 Amidst much speculation about Heathcliff's roots is a suggestion that he might be Irish. Certainly, in the context of the famine in which the novel was first read, the figure of a starving child from the Liverpool docks would necessarily have suggested that connection. Interestingly, there are few mainstream fictional references beyond this of Heathcliff to the famine in Ireland. There is perhaps, as Terry Eagleton suggests in *Heathcliff and the Great Hunger* (London, 1995), something unassimilable in the force of nature which the famine constitutes.

32 Michael Holquist writes that 'Novelness is the name Bakhtin gives to a form of knowledge that can most powerfully put different orders of experience – each of whose languages claims authority on the basis of its ability to exclude others – into dialogue with each other' (*Dialogism: Bakhtin and His World* (London, 1990), p. 87).

33 Martin Daunton, 'Society and Economic Life', in Colin Matthew, ed., *The Nineteenth Century, 1815–1901* (Oxford, 2000), pp. 41–82 (p. 42). Details of the 1851 Census are also taken from this source.

34 For further details of the Shilling Days, and for the way in which the Great Exhibition initiated a commodity culture in Britain, see Chapter 1, 'The Great Exhibition of Things', in Thomas Richards, *The Commodity Culture of Victorian England: Advertising and Spectacle, 1851–1914* (London, 1991), pp. 17–72.

35 John Ruskin, 'The Nature of Gothic', in Clive Wilmer, ed., *John Ruskin: Unto This Last and Other Writings*, pp. 75–109 (p. 87).

36 Quoted in Tim Hilton, *John Ruskin: The Early Years* (New Haven, 1985), p. 157.

37 Despite the continuing growth in population (the British population rose by more than 10 per cent in every decade from 1781 to 1911 (Hoppen, *The Mid-Victorian Generation*, p. 279)), and the provision of statistics which might have provided the basis of welfare reform, government intervention at this period was limited to a very few measures which would secure the health and safety of industry as well as the nation, such as the Compulsory Vaccination Act (1853) which was an attempt to stop the spread of smallpox (the disease which besets Esther Summerson in *Bleak House* (1852–53)) among children, then a significant part of the work-force. Further, in 1856, the basis of a national police force was laid down when government insisted on co-ordination between different local forces.

38 The work was originally published in 1835, and was translated into English by Mary Ann Evans, later better known as George Eliot, in 1846.

39 There is, of course, also another layer of conflict and division within religious practice at the time between the Established Anglican church and the dissenting denominations. However, this friction was of long standing. What concerns us here is the distinctive emergence in this period of the challenge to faith per se, rather than to specific forms of practice and belief.

40 Elisabeth Jay, *Faith and Doubt in Victorian Britain* (Basingstoke, 1986), p. 72.

41 R. Gilmour, *The Intellectual and Cultural Context of English Literature, 1830–1890* (Harlow, 1993), p. 72.

42 Charles Dickens, *Bleak House* (Harmondsworth, 1971), p. 724, ch. 47.

43 As one might expect, Ruskin thoroughly approved of *Hard Times*, and in a note to the first essay of *Unto This Last*, his attack on political economy, which was first published in the *Cornhill Magazine* in 1860, he writes that the novel 'should be studied with close and earnest care by persons interested in social questions'. He does, however, wish that Dickens might 'limit his brilliant exaggeration to works written only for public amusement', as his caricatures often obscure the truth of his view (Wilmer, *Ruskin*, p. 171).

44 J.R. McCulloch, *The Principles of Political Economy* (1830), quoted in the critical apparatus of Charles Dickens, *Hard Times* (New York and London, 1990), pp. 321–2.

45 Interestingly, in his *Household Words* article on the Preston strike, Dickens is much more generous to the union than he is in *Hard Times*, speaking in his journalism of their 'astonishing fortitude and perseverance', and of the dignified way in which the agitator 'Gruffshaw' is put down ('On Strike' [11 February 1854], in David Pascoe, ed., *Charles Dickens: Selected Journalism, 1850–1870* (Harmondsworth, 1997), pp. 452–66 (p. 463).

46 Earl Grey, Colonial Secretary, speaking in 1848, quoted in Ronald Hyam, *Britain's Imperial Century, 1815–1914* (Basingstoke, 2nd edn, 1993), p. 43.

47 For details of Woolner's emigration and Brown's painting, see Tim Barringer, *The Pre-Raphaelites* (London, 1998), pp. 86–9.

48 For further details, see Philippa Levine, *Victorian Feminism, 1850–1900* (London, 1987), pp. 135–6.

49 For their responses, and a survey of reviews of the novel, see Helsinger, Sheets, and Veeder, *The Woman Question*, pp. 113–22.

50 Charles Dickens, 'An Appeal to Fallen Women', in Kate Flint, ed., *The Victorian Novelist: Social Problems and Social Change* (London, 1987), pp. 134–6 (p. 135). The 'original' behind Ruth was also bound for the colonies (see

Deborah Epstein Nord, *Walking the Victorian Streets: Women, Representation and the City* (Ithaca and London, 1995), pp. 164–5).

51 *Mrs Warren's Profession* was written in 1893, published in 1898, but not publicly performed in Britain until 1926. In it, Bernard Shaw reveals the economic grounds forcing women into prostitution, and the moral complexities that the prostitute provokes.

52 Elizabeth Gaskell, *North and South* (Harmondsworth, 1970), p. 233, ch. 22.

|2|

1856–1870
Questions of identity

During this period, many of the buildings that seem to us now to represent the epitome of Victorian self-confidence were being built. In Leeds, Cuthbert Brodrick's grandiose Town Hall was opened in 1858, and Manchester's Gothic Town Hall, designed by Alfred Waterhouse, was begun in 1867. London saw the erection of George Gilbert Scott's Foreign Office (1862–73), his Albert Memorial (1863–72), and St Pancras Station (1867). Outwardly, then, and economically, the period was one of prosperity and the appearance of confirmed progress, where a surplus of wealth was available for the creation of a civic culture and new civic spaces both in London and in the newly confident industrial cities of the north. However, this was also a period in which, due to developments in politics and science, and conflicts in Britain's colonies, considerable anxieties began to be felt about the fundamental grounds upon which identity, both national and individual, was founded. It is, then, an awkward time, a kind of Victorian adolescence, in which public activities seem designed often to act as bulwarks against the encroaching uncertainties of modernity, and in which discourse lags behind the realities with which it must grapple, when the uncertainties necessarily attendant upon any form of movement or progress seem certain to upset the benefits thus derived.

The evolutionary hypothesis

We begin with Britain in the midst of the Crimean War (1854–56). Notable mainly for showing up significant failings in the supply and administration of the army, and hence providing material for Dickens's parody of the aristocratically and nepotistically staffed Circumlocution Office in *Little Dorrit* (1855–57), the Crimea is an apt introduction to a period in which the

concept of the struggle for survival spread beyond its immediate application
to situations of war or poverty, and was hypothesized as a necessary
condition of existence. The telegraph (and the previously unseen immediacy
of journalism from the front lines) meant that the public were allowed
access to the confusion and bungling of the Crimea, to the suffering, disease
and bravery of their soldiers, and to the work of Florence Nightingale. They
were thus provided with the language and visceral images of struggle which
were to permeate the work of scientists and political analysts, and which
would inevitably echo also within fiction. In *The Origin of Species* (1859),
Charles Darwin writes of the struggle for existence as a 'war of nature', in
which man was fully implicated.[1] He provides the scientific backing for
Malthus's theories of population growth and control, from which indeed
Darwin derived his 'crucial insight into the mechanism of evolutionary
change',[2] and involves man in an inter-species competition for the resources
of survival.

Unlike today's scientific advances, the works of Darwin and his fellow
scientists were readily available to a general readership, partly because
science had not yet developed the specialized language it now employs, and
were made readily available through the medium of the periodical publications which reviewed scientific writings along with other new publications. The early and mid-nineteenth century saw something of a popular
cult of amateur scientists, including in fiction Gaskell's Roger Hamley in
Wives and Daughters (1864–66) and George Eliot's Mr Farebrother in
Middlemarch. Both novels are set in the early 1830s, the period which saw
the beginnings of the narrative of geological discovery which would
eventually lead to Darwin. Lyell's *Principles of Geology*, and more
especially Robert Chambers's *Vestiges of the Natural History of Creation*
(1844) provided a scientifically literate and enthusiastic audience with the
first suggestions that the evidence of geology might contradict the creation
narrative of Genesis, its time-span necessarily predicating a far longer
history for the world than the Bible allowed. Darwin's major contribution
to the evolutionary hypothesis was that he provided a mechanism for the
changes perceived, whereas his forerunners had only given evidence of
change. In his theory of natural selection, whereby the most favourable
variations, the fittest, of a species survive while others perish, he emphatic-
ally made 'the Creator' a redundant entity in the face of the operation of
natural laws. It was arguably religious belief which was the most immediate
casualty of Darwin's work, as the scientist replaced the priest as the source
of ontological explanation. In this context Anthony Trollope's Barsetshire
and Margaret Oliphant's Carlingford series of clerical novels come to seem
both nostalgic as well as interrogative.[3]

Darwin's theory also entailed a new understanding of history and its processes, substituting for theories of catastrophism and revolution in nature the more gradual process of evolutionary transformation, which needed more than one life-time in which to be seen. As Sally Shuttleworth points out, the conclusion to George Eliot's *The Mill on the Floss* (1860) explores the different implications of these alternatives in offering the reader two possible interpretations of its ending.[4] In one, 'Nature repairs her ravages – repairs them with her sunshine, and with human labour', and life goes on, the Floss becoming again the host to 'wharves and warehouses'. But not all nature's ravages are repaired: 'The uptorn trees are not rooted again – the parted hills are left scarred.'[5] One reading enables nature's actions to become part of a cycle of destruction and re-birth, the other to be a perpetually rupturing experience from which there is no return. Its meaning is resolutely end-stopped. *The Origin of Species* rather confutes the latter understanding, as the text itself concludes:

> from the war of nature, from famine and death, the most exalted object which we are capable of conceiving, namely, the production of the higher animals, directly follows. There is grandeur in this view of life, with its several powers, having been originally breathed into a few forms or into one; and that, whilst this planet has gone cycling on according to the fixed law of gravity, from so simple a beginning endless forms most beautiful and most wonderful have been, and are being, evolved.
>
> (pp. 459–60)

The wonder of creation is still extant, albeit subject to fixed laws, but, as Gillian Beer notes, there is now no ending (Beer, *Darwin's Plots*, p. 64). (See extract 2, p. 137.) Evolution is an ongoing narrative which sends its strands out into an unknown future, thus categorically denying the fixity of closure of some fiction, and indeed of the signifying power of endings, which give meaning to what has gone before. As Beer writes, 'Evolutionary ideas shifted in very diverse ways the patterns through which we apprehend experience and hence the patterns through which we condense experience in the telling of it' (*Darwin's Plots*, p. 8).

Man's privileged place within narrative was also ineluctably disturbed by Darwin's writings. There was no provision for the individual within the evolutionary struggle of species, and no place for any intimation of a soul. There was, further, no guarantee that man was, as had been supposed, the best-developed life-species. In the new narrative authored by Darwin, man might represent just one stage in the progress to new and better forms. In 1892, A.E. Housman said of man that he was:

in the position of one who has been reared from the cradle as the child of a noble race and the heir to great possessions, and who finds at his coming of age that he has been deceived alike as to his origins and his expectations.[6]

A more contemporary expression of the same feeling might be found in Dickens's *Great Expectations*, where this feeling of a new form of post-lapsarian grief is transposed into a more conventional narrative of Pip's disappointed expectations of social progress.

Darwin's claim that man was descended from apes was, however, the aspect of his work which raised most contemporary controversy, and was one of the main bones of contention between Darwin's champion T.H. Huxley and Bishop Wilberforce at a crucial meeting of the British Association for the Advancement of Science at Oxford in 1860. Charles Kingsley's *The Water Babies* parodies evolutionary descent from apes by reversing it, in a text which seeks to confute Darwin by arguing for an intrinsically moral form of progression. And in Wilkie Collins's *The Law and the Lady* (1875) man's descent from animals is, for the old family clerk Benjamin, the final absurdity in the confusions of the modern age:

> Let's go and get crammed with ready-made science at a lecture – let's hear the last new professor, the man who has been behind the scenes at Creation, and knows to a T how the world was made, and how long it took to make it. There's the other fellow, too: mind we don't forget the modern Solomon who has left his proverbs behind him – the bran-new philosopher who considers the consolations of religion in the light of harmless playthings, and who is kind enough to say that he might have been all the happier if he could only have been childish enough to play with them himself. Oh, the new ideas, the new ideas, what consoling, elevating, beautiful discoveries have been made by the new ideas! We were all monkeys before we were men, and molecules before we were monkeys![7]

As we will see, the impact of Darwin is variously felt throughout the nineteenth century, achieving perhaps its darkest implications in the degenerative theories of the 1890s, but it is already clear that Darwin's writings crystallized a paradigm shift in man's understanding of the world and of his own place within it. This was in part because the concerns of *The Origin of Species* worked in a powerful synchronicity with other pressing concerns of the time. Most disturbingly perhaps, and in line with what we have learnt of the workings of political economy in the mid-nineteenth century, Darwin's version of the evolutionary hypothesis was one devoid of moral considerations. Natural selection worked with all the impersonality of a machine. It was also a theory which fed into debates about progress, notably by denying its presence in the development of life from simple into more complex forms: this was simply part of the law by which evolution worked.[8]

And, of course, evolution fundamentally altered concepts of individuality and identity, mirroring in this respect developments in the new field of psychology. Alongside evolutionary theory, the influence of psychology was widely felt both in the society and fiction of the period, for like Darwin's work it fundamentally altered concepts of identity and individuality. Darwin's work impinged on concepts of man as a social and spiritual being. Psychological writings concerned themselves with memory, sexual desire, madness, and the mind–body relationship, but were perhaps most important in adding the dimension of the unconscious to the possibility of human identity.

Psychology and the sensation novel

The intervention of psychological theories in fiction was not unique to this period, for the realm of the mind, and debates over its various states, had been concerning novelists for some time. But in the 1860s new conditions prevailed. The potential readership for fiction, which was expanding rapidly, was better informed about developments in psychology than had been its predecessors. The popularity of works like *Chambers's Encyclopaedia: A Dictionary of Universal Knowledge for the People* (a new edition of which was issued between 1860 and 1868) and William Carpenter's widely read *Principles of Human Physiology* (which went into a fourth edition in 1853, and a fifth only two years later), meant that there was an informed appetite for fiction which explored states of consciousness. There were also, of course, in the 1860s, the new feelings of uncertainty and curiosity as to origins and identities which had been created by the work of evolutionary scientists. In 1867, Francis Power Cobbe articulates the effects of this unsettling feeling:

> On our generation of mankind has come the knowledge of an isolation, such as younger races never felt, and perhaps could less have borne. ... Science, as she marches round us in wider and yet wider circles, leaves ever a hard and barren track behind her, on which no flower of fancy may bloom again. And at this hour she tells, or threatens to tell us yet more – that if we would know the parents from

whom we came, whose Paradise-home yet seems the cradle of our
infancy, we must retrace the world's course not for six thousand years,
but for ages of millenniums, and find them at last – not beautiful and
calm, conversing in Eden with the sons of God – but simious-browed
and dwarf of limb, struggling with the mammoth and the cave-bear in
the howling wilderness of an uncultured world.[9]

It was precisely these anxieties about inheritance, memory, identity, that the
'sensation' novel of the 1860s was well placed to exploit, explore, and
finally try to calm, and, in so doing, it invested heavily in the new discourses
of popular psychology.

In its narratives of bigamy, illegitimacy, theft, madness, and mistaken
identity, the sensation novel used the psychological element, most notably
that of the unconscious, to underpin its element of suspense, and add a
new dimension to the mystery that had inevitably to be solved. The
reassuring detective–narrator figure, in whose hands all eventually comes
right, investigates not only empirical clues, but also the states of mind of
protagonists, which figure as a parallel mystery narrative. The figure of
the detective himself is not exempt, however, from investigation, as his
own state of mind becomes part of the case-study that the reader is to
investigate. In *The Woman in White* (1859–60) for instance, Walter
Hartright's mind is itself subject to the accusations of monomania which
he detects in Anne Catherick, the eponymous woman in white, and his
processes of deduction are evidence of the 'unconscious cerebration'
which Carpenter and Cobbe postulated in the 1850s and 1860s. Meanings inaccessible to reason become available through the freeing of the
unconscious in dreams, or in chains of thought working independently of
any conscious control in their 'host', and thus the detective has to work
also to create a narrative linking, and making sense of, making safe, the
recesses of the mind. *The Woman in White* unravels two mysteries, that of
Sir Percival Glyde's secret (his being illegitimate, and thus having no claim
to his father's estate), and of Anne Catherick's paternity. However, alongside these ostensibly primary concerns run anxieties over Laura Fairlie's
and Anne Catherick's states of mind, and their incarceration in an asylum;
Count Fosco's apparently mesmeric powers; and the fragility of the mind,
for more characters than Frederick Fairlie are subject to the debilitating
effects of mental stress.

The question of identity is integral to this as to other sensation fictions.
Mistaken identity, hidden identities, are the staple of Collins's *No Name*
(1862) and *Armadale* (1866), and Mary Braddon's *Lady Audley's Secret*
(1862), and are often concerned with questions of inheritance, with legal

identity, but the language of psychology allowed other dimensions of the question to be addressed. What precisely constitutes identity comes into question as the workings of memory are investigated, and found to be lacking. Since John Locke, the continuity of memory, and access to it, had been considered a safeguard of stable, knowable identity. In *An Essay Concerning Human Understanding* (1690), Locke argues that:

> since consciousness always accompanies thinking, and it is that that makes everyone to be what he calls 'self' . . . as far as his consciousness can be extended backwards to any past action or thought, so far reaches the identity of that person.
>
> (Book 2, ch. 27, para. 9)

However, Cobbe argues, and sensation novels demonstrate, that memory is rather:

> a finger-mark traced on shifting sand, ever exposed to obliteration when left unnerved; and if renewed then modified, and made, not the same, but a fresh and different mark. Beyond the first time of recalling a place or event, it is rare to remember again actually the place or event. . . . We find, indeed, in our minds something which we call a remembrance, and which appertains in truth to the faculty of memory; but it reproduces, not the event it assumes to record, but that idea of it which, after twenty modifying repetitions, has left for the moment the uppermost trace in our minds.[10]

As evolution had reduced collective memory to inherited instincts, so psychology questioned the individual's basis of identity in memory.

The interrogations of psychology, and its probing of the stability of individual identity, are just one part of the sensation novel's broader investigation into what Henry James called 'the mysteries which are at our own doors'.[11] Indeed, it was rather with what lay inside these doors that the sensation novel was most concerned. The constitution of home and family are the staple of the sensation novel, and their dissolution and reconstitution its basic plot. In *No Name*, the happiness of the Vanstone home is shown to be built around unmarried parents, and the whole dissolves into a narrative of the anguish of the children's illegitimacy, before finally being restored in those children's own legitimate married homes. In its concern with the fragile domestic space, seen again in Audley Court, where the ageing Sir Michael builds a domestic fantasy around the new Lady Audley, a bigamist and would-be murderess, the sensation novel was exploiting contemporary events, such as the Divorce Act of 1857, and attendant journalism, which exposed the secret workings of the home and its weaknesses. The domestic space also figured largely in the theatre of the 1860s, as companies, like that led by Squire and Marie Bancroft, used the trappings of the home, such as pot plants and anti-macassars, within their theatres to diminish the gap between the domestic and theatrical experience, and thus to make their auditoria more welcoming and respectable for middle-class audiences. On-stage too, the home was invoked in the so-called 'cup and saucer' dramas of Tom Robertson, such as *Society* (1865), *Caste* (1867), and *School* (1869), which were acted in a newly intimate style, and were described by Henry James as 'among the most diminutive experiments ever attempted in the drama'.[12]

The theatrical metaphor is used to great effect in Victorian novels, and nowhere more so than in the sensation novel, a sub-genre having much in common with the popular theatre. Having been cast on her own resources to earn a living, *No Name*'s Magdalen Vanstone takes briefly to the stage (before using her acting abilities to woo her cousin Noel Vanstone, the recipient of her father's legacy). On it, she appears in a one-woman *tour de force* in which she plays 'A Young Lady at Home'.[13] Provided with 'appropriate dresses', 'her accomplishments in singing and playing' well developed, and with 'plenty of smart talk addressed to the audience' (p. 191), she was essentially acting out the part of the legitimate young middle-class woman whom she had previously believed herself to be. In an earlier stage appearance, she had mimicked her sister Nora's characteristics. The text suggests that Magdalen has betrayed something of herself in these performances, and has compromised her femininity and dignity. However, what she really exposes is that that very femininity and dignity may themselves be assumed, may be masquerades, rather than the naturally occurring, transparently available phenomena they were believed to be. Hearth and home are rendered vulnerable as the femininity which guarantees their sanctity is revealed as a performance.

This is particularly the case in Braddon's *Lady Audley's Secret*, an instant best-seller, and a novel which went on to be successful in stage adaptations too. Its heroine, Lucy, is the much younger second wife of Sir Michael Audley, and seems to epitomize a domestic ideal. Skilled in painting and music:

> Wherever she went she seemed to take joy and brightness with her. . . .
> Every one loved, admired, and praised her. The boy who opened the
> five-barred gate that stood in her pathway ran home to his mother to
> tell of her pretty looks, and the sweet voice in which she thanked him
> for the little service.[14]

However, Lucy Audley is really Helen Talboys, abandoned wife of George Talboys and mother of a small child. Her decision to marry the doting Sir

Michael is taken on strictly economic grounds. Their house is therefore founded on criminal deceit and financial concern, not love, and it has to be sustained by attempted murder, arson, and a string of lies when Helen's husband returns to reclaim his young wife. Her virtues and her home are illusions, created for her own ends of survival. This might be deeply threatening for a contemporary readership were it not for the get-out clause which Braddon, like Collins, offers her readers. Rather than assume Helen/Lucy to be not untypical of any woman who has her living to think about, and who might mimic acceptable femininity to get that living, Braddon minimizes her heroine's disruptive powers by suggesting that she has been certifiably mad all along, that her actions are the result of a disordered mind, and not simply of a woman's awareness of what she must do to survive, and of the terms upon which her survival can be purchased.

If we look to another, non-sensation, text of the time, however, we can see the threat of self-consciousness embodied by Lady Audley, and the actress, being fulfilled there too. Mrs Beeton's *Book of Household Management* (1859–61) is far from being simply a recipe book. It not only carries intimate teaching on the running of the middle-class home, but also instructs the mistress of the home in those matters of feelings and manners which were usually supposed to come naturally to women of a certain class. Instructions on making conversation (and whether or not light needlework may be continued while speaking) and making friends mingle with the correct use of finger-glasses, the need to avoid the French practice of gargling at the table, and the importance of good drains. The mistress of the house is, 'the first and last, the Alpha and the Omega in the government of her establishment; and . . . it is by her conduct that its whole internal policy is regulated'.[15] This last thought reveals the grounds which are at stake in women's dereliction of their domestic duties, and why it was deemed necessary that such books as Beeton's needed to be written. However, it does also reveal that it should no longer be assumed that women were naturally domestically competent, nor necessarily interested primarily in the home: Mrs Beeton is very strict about the necessity of curtailing outside amusements, lest the home should suffer by neglect. Sensation fiction allows the reader to enjoy the spectacle of women exploring non-domestic aspects of their lives, safe in the knowledge that the highly conventional genre will eventually re-erect the walls of the home around its heroines, or put her instead into an asylum.

Outside the realms of fiction, women were pushing still further against the boundaries of expectation and tradition. In 1863 they were allowed to take Cambridge local examinations, and in 1868 the first exams for women were set by London University. In 1869 and 1870 respectively the institutions that would become Girton and Newnham colleges in Cambridge were founded, thus providing dedicated higher education for women. In medicine, too, provision for training was extended by the Nightingale School of Nursing (1860), and the establishment of a college of midwives in 1865. It was also in this decade that Elizabeth Blackwell and Elizabeth Garrett became the first women to qualify as doctors. The question of the suffrage, of concern in the run-up to the second Reform Act of 1867, was extended to women as suffrage societies were set up in London, Edinburgh, Birmingham, and Bristol. In 1866, John Stuart Mill presented an unsuccessful petition for women's suffrage to parliament, and followed this up in 1869 with the publication of *The Subjection of Women*, which stressed the artificiality of the women being produced by society's dictates. Outside parliament, women (when ratepayers) became eligible to vote in municipal elections (in 1869), and to stand for election to local school boards (in 1870).

They also achieved a political voice through organized agitation against the Contagious Diseases Acts (passed in 1864, 1866, and 1869). These Acts were concerned to protect the sexual health of the armed forces.[16] Rather than try to police the army and navy, however, it was decided that anyone suspected of being a prostitute in a garrison town might be examined, and subsequently forcibly detained should treatment for a disease be necessary. In 1869, the Ladies' National Association for the Repeal of the Contagious Diseases Acts was formed, and proved both energetic and explicit in its protests against the double standards and class prejudices enshrined in the laws. The Association was also crucial in confirming women's knowledge of sexual matters, and in publicizing that knowledge. Michel Foucault writes of modern societies, including the Victorian, that they are peculiar not in that they 'consigned sex to a shadow existence, but that they dedicated themselves to speaking of it *ad infinitum*, while exploiting it as *the* secret'.[17] We can see, then, that many of the secrets around which sensation fiction was based, concerning women's knowledge of matters sexual and criminal, were in fact rather open secrets, made illicit for the sake of gripping fiction rather than verisimilitude.

In fact, many women were doing all they could to expose the double standard which constrained them, and which could only persist if women were ignorant of or compliant with its premises. In a notorious article of 1868 by Eliza Lynn Linton, the country's first professional female journalist but also one of the greatest opponents of liberated women, the 'Girl of the Period' is berated as a 'loud and rampant modernization with her false red hair and painted skin, talking slang as glibly as a man, and by preference leading the conversation to doubtful subjects'.[18] The Girl's greatest offences are in seeking to be autonomous and in blurring the lines between the respectable woman and the demi-mondaine. The Girl, with her make-up and dyed hair, threatens with her knowing and her appropriation of the tricks of sexual attraction, just as do the penetrating, often immodest, gazes of the heroines of Rossetti's paintings of this period, such as his 'Monna Vanna' (1866) and 'Pandora' (1869). Ruskin's much-maligned essay 'Of Queens' Gardens' was insistent in its praise of the 'true wife', and of her incorruptible goodness, her infallible wisdom, and her intellect, which 'is not for invention or creation, but for sweet ordering, arangement, and decision'.[19] Ruskin argues passionately, and accords to women a tremendous dignity in limited circumstances, but most notable of all is the feeling that Ruskin is writing against the tide of current trends, that women have to be enjoined to be good wives because they are now so ready to behave in new and unprecedented ways.

Us and them: Britain and its colonies

In 1857, Thomas Hughes opened his *Tom Brown's Schooldays* with a chapter in praise of the Browns, a family held to represent the essence of unremarkable British virtue and diligence: 'For centuries, in their quiet, dogged, homespun way, they have been subduing the earth in most English counties, and leaving their mark in American forests and Australian uplands'.[20] Their efforts at subduing the earth are not, however, restricted to agriculture, as Hughes goes on to suggest in writing of 'the great army of Browns, who are scattered over the whole empire on which the sun never sets, and whose general diffusion I take to be the chief cause of that empire's stability' (p. 5). The family's function and identity are ineluctably bound up with the possession of colonies, as is the identity of the nation as a whole.

In many of the novels referred to so far, the idea of Empire has not figured prominently, but has nevertheless been a fundamental part of the economic and moral fabric of the fictional worlds conjured up. The domestic Gothic drama of *Jane Eyre* interrogates the metaphor of slavery and applies it to women as it moves from Jane's repudiation of the 'rebel slave' label for herself, through a consideration of Bertha's origins and incarceration, into its depiction of the freedoms won for Jane by the inheritance of colonial riches from her uncle. The novel also of course ends by sending St John Rivers off to India to be a missionary, one of the most important means of extending the nineteenth-century Empire. The industrial novels silently rely upon India as a market and source for textiles, as well as the provenance of the 'Indian shawls' which are the most prized possession of fictional heroines, including Edith in *North and South*:

Helen had set her heart upon an Indian shawl, but really when I found what an extravagant price was asked, I refused her. She will be quite envious when she hears of Edith having Indian shawls. What kinds are they? Delhi? with the lovely little borders?

(pp. 37–8, ch. 1)

They are the ultimate luxury to be brought back by sons like Jos Sedley (in *Vanity Fair*) and appropriately gloss, while displaying the economic terms upon which relations between the colonies and Britain were based.

At this period, much of the colonizing effort was carried on by individuals (including missionaries and settlers) and companies rather than by the state. Free trade rather than intervention was seen as the most appropriate means of extending and maintaining Britain's sway. Thus, the colonies become another branch of the domestic market place, albeit one to which the extension of that influence is enabled because of inherent beliefs about the inferiority of the peoples to be encompassed under British sway. The metaphor of the child crops up frequently in writings about India and Africa at this period, a metaphor which enables the extension of the arm of benevolent paternalism and maturity from Britain. As Patrick Brantlinger suggests in his *Rule of Darkness: British Literature and Imperialism, 1830–1914*, the experience of colonial power gradually came to be a self-validating one for the British.[21] Much then was at stake in the colonial enterprise: moral status, economic power, and the nation's self-respect rested upon its maintenance of a healthy Empire. However, in 1857, the Indian Mutiny occurred, an event which, in the first instance, seemed to threaten to undermine that Empire.

The immediate impetus to mutiny came with the provision of gun cartridges which were lubricated with cow and pig fat and which were thus equally offensive to Hindu (for whom the cow was sacred) and Muslim (for whom the pig was unclean) soldiers. The imprisonment of soldiers refusing to use the cartridges led to the sympathetic uprising of a cavalry regiment in Meerut near Delhi, and thus a rebellion was sparked which spread, albeit unevenly, throughout the country. The make-up of the army in India, only 45,552 out of 277,746 of whom were Europeans, meant that complete overthrow of English power was initially a real possibility. Indeed, the Mutiny was only quashed after 14 months of fighting. However, the geographical and social extent of the rebellion suggested that its causes were far more complex and of longer standing than a military dispute over greased cartridges. Rebellion was fiercest where other cultural norms and indigenous practices had been violated.[22]

Disraeli noted in a speech to parliament in July 1857 that 'of late years':

> Laws and manners, customs and usages, political organisations, the tenure of property, the religion of the people – everything in India has either been changed or attempted to be changed, or there is a suspicion among the population that a desire for change exists on the part of our Government.
>
> (quoted in Porter, *The Lion's Share*, p. 31)

Overzealous missionaries ostracized both Hindus and Muslims, and humanitarian reforms, such as the abolition of suttee, the education of women, higher education based in English, and equality before the law for all Indians, offended traditional customs and beliefs, and most specifically often disregarded the rules of caste. The artisan class had been economically destroyed by free trade with England and the import of manufactured goods. Most significantly, and ironically perhaps in view of the reverence accorded to land by the English landowner, the British had interfered with practices of land tenure and inheritance. As many novels of the period demonstrate, questions of inheritance dominate family relations, marriage settlements, and the politics of country towns, and land was the most visceral form of legacy and the most potent sign of power. The British in India disregarded all they knew of the sacredness of landownership in their attempts to systematize tenure in India. Land was confiscated from families who had worked it for centuries in the absence of documentary proof of ownership; princes' estates passed into the government's hands as they abolished the practice of allowing princes without sons to adopt heirs; and land taxes, the largest form of government revenue, were often sufficiently severe to drive farmers off their land.

The Mutiny was eventually quashed, and a new regime in India instated which involved much more direct government control, and the curbing of the more zealous 'reformers'. Culturally, the impact of the Mutiny seems to have been to enforce a rigidly dichotomized notion of the fundamental differences between Indian and British identities. In thus rebelling, the Indians had proved their need of firm, paternalistic government from overseas. Furthermore, in the various atrocities they committed in the course of the Mutiny, they had proved their inalienable otherness from the British. The most notorious of such atrocities was the so-called Massacre at Cawnpore, where women and children, who had previously been guaranteed safe passage out of the town, were attacked as they were leaving for Allahabad, with any survivors being first imprisoned, and then hacked

to death and their bodies thrown into a well. British atrocities were of
course also rife, and the slaughter of many thousands of Indians in
Allahabad probably led to the Cawnpore events, but their lack of press
coverage meant that the well at Cawnpore could become the defining image
of Indian turpitude in the many popular novels, plays, and historical
accounts of the Mutiny.

As Patrick Brantlinger notes, these texts put into operation the full workings of the dehumanizing practice of 'Orientalism' identified by Edward
Said, which demonizes and dehumanizes the Eastern other. They also show
a morbid and repellent fascination with the tales of sexual atrocity which
emerged out of the Mutiny, and which give a perverse justification for the
brutal suppression of the Indians, and the subsequent and more significant
removal of their humanity. In the years following the Mutiny, then, the
British government and nation found in India not so much a source of
challenge to British rule, and to the identity of the male members of the
imperial Brown family, but rather an arena in which that identity might now
be more forcibly reinscribed, and where the recent challenges of domestic
politics and developments might be disregarded. In India, as popular fiction
and the Cawnpore massacre showed, women were to be protected and
nurtured, not feared for their political ambitions. Religious missionaries had
new fields to explore in their quest for conversion, and in the 1860s were at
their most prominent at precisely the time when religious belief was being
severely challenged at home. They were able to take advantage of the newly
subsidized schools in India, and new access to China following the end of
the second Opium War in 1860. Furthermore, in the colonies the effect of
Darwin's work was less painfully felt. Indeed, in this context, the evolutionary hypothesis could be enrolled to bolster the colonizers' significance. The
evolutionary scheme might seem to justify both that pre-eminence and the
necessity of the presence of the white government to a home nation for
whom the Indian was less noble than purely savage. These effects extended
also to Africa, for his work in which continent Livingstone became a
national hero. His *Missionary Travels* sold 70,000 copies within months of
its 1857 publication (Brantlinger, *Rule of Darkness*, p. 180), and he became
an adventure hero, starring in his own quest narrative. The discovery of
quinine in 1859 enabled further explorations in Africa, which subsequently
led to the discovery of the source of the Nile in 1862.

Little of these developments make their way into the fiction that we now
read from the late 1850s and 1860s, despite the fact that, as Hilda Gregg
writes in 1897, 'of all the great events of this century, as they are reflected in
fiction, the Indian Mutiny has taken the firmest hold on the popular imagination' (quoted in Brantlinger, *Rule of Darkness*, p. 199). Distasteful as they

would be to modern readers, none of the Mutiny novels has been reclaimed by recent scholars in the field of Victorian fiction. But the issue begs the question of why these events do not figure more largely in more 'canonical' works. It might have been the case that at this time other genres, such as memoirs, journalism, and travel writing, satisfied the appetite for stories which were essentially of the moment, and which received part of their attraction by the very speed with which they were transmitted from the front line of events. As we will see, Africa did later come to take a prominent place in the adventure and quest fiction of the 1880s, when the so-called 'Scramble for Africa' between European nations began, and when contemporary anxieties about masculinity and fiction itself demanded their reinvigoration through virile stories of African subjugation. But, for much of the 1860s, fiction rather performed its colonial purpose by silently integrating the artefacts and processes of colonialism into its text as phenomena sufficiently natural not to deserve remark.

By the end of the decade, however, a range of legislative measures and continuing disturbances in Ireland, a 'colonial' nation close to home, encouraged novelists to acknowledge the interventionist methods of imperialism. The Jamaica Crisis of 1865, in which, in response to a relatively limited uprising prompted by settlers' unauthorized annexation of land, the Governor, and former explorer, Edward Eyre, had 439 blacks hanged, at least 600 more flogged, and many of their homes burned, also forced Britain to confront its colonial identity. The hangings took five weeks to complete after the outbreak was contained.[23] Opinion in England was divided between those who found the official response barbarous and inexcusable, and those who believed any measure justified in the interest of preventing more widespread unrest. Disturbingly for modern readers, Dickens, Tennyson, Kingsley, and Ruskin lined up in support of Governor Eyre. As Suvendrini Perera notes, the controversy forced upon England the necessity of considering 'the nature of the necessary relationship between domestic and imperial actions',[24] and prompted novelists to interrogate the metaphors, means and implications, psychological, sexual, and cultural, of the recognition of that relationship. In doing so, Wilkie Collins's *The Moonstone* (1868) and Dickens's unfinished *The Mystery of Edwin Drood* (1870) concentrate on the East, and on the opium which was one of India's most significant exports to Britain.[25]

In both novels, opium has the effect of exposing a form of double consciousness in those taking it, and thus of uncovering hidden or submerged motives, and repressed desires. Dickens's John Jasper repeatedly enacts what the reader assumes to be the murder of his nephew Edwin Drood during his spells in the London opium den in which the novel begins. And in *The Moonstone* opium is put to a more innocent, experimental use in seeking to uncover actions which escape the conscious mind. In both texts, however, the opium acts metonymically to suggest a whole society operating in wilful ignorance of its own doubleness, as it acted in wilful ignorance of the imperial activities and atrocities upon which domestic prosperity rested. Dickens's Miss Twinkleton, head of one of Cloisterham's two schools for young ladies, has 'two distinct and separate phases of being',[26] one sprightly and social, the other professional and scholastic, each of which depends on manifest ignorance of the other. Politically, too, opium exposed the fallacy of the notion of Britain's adopting a free trade policy overseas. The so-called Opium Wars of 1839 and 1859–60 were prompted by Britain's desire to continue paying for its tea with Indian opium, which the Chinese government had forbidden, and by its wish to increase trading opportunities in China. When the government intervened by going to war with China, they were in effect admitting that 'free trade' was unfeasible.

Through the person of John Jasper, opium infiltrates into the heart of English respectability, the Cathedral close, also notably the subject of investigation in Trollope's Barsetshire novels. In the delirious vision of 'the ancient English Cathedral town' which opens *The Mystery of Edwin Drood*, the 'well-known massive grey square tower of its old Cathedral' mingles in the air with a 'spike of rusty iron' which may have been:

> set up by the Sultan's orders for the impaling of a horde of Turkish robbers, one by one. It is so, for cymbals clash, and the Sultan goes by to his palace in long procession. Ten thousand scimitars flash in the sunlight, and thrice ten thousand dancing-girls strew flowers. Then follow white elephants caparisoned in gorgeous colours, and infinite in number and attendants.

> (p. 37)

Through Jasper, the fear of the colonies is unleashed within Cloisterham, though he is skilled enough to turn that fear upon Neville Landless, newly arrived from Ceylon, and admitting himself to having imbibed something of the 'tigerish' (p. 90, ch. 7) blood of that nation. Neville, around whom images of darkness cluster, and who is automatically the strongest suspect for the murder of Edwin Drood, is in many ways an idealized colonial subject, self-policing and self-repressing, and evidently benefiting from the instruction of the minor canon and English embodiment of the advantages of hearty exercise, Septimus Crisparkle. Nonetheless, he is driven out of Cloisterham, a town which seems to feel the need to maintain Neville's colonized status by meeting him with violence and suspicion.

Neville's greatest foe is Edwin Drood, who represents the complacency of the imperial state in his professed intention shortly to 'wake up Egypt a little' (p. 96, ch. 8), when he goes there as part of the engineering enterprise that resulted in the opening of the Suez Canal in 1869,[27] a triumph of engineering, which would, as Edwin confidently predicts to Rosa, 'change the whole condition of an undeveloped country' (p. 59, ch. 3). That he regards her also as a country awaiting judicious development is made abundantly clear. Sexual and colonial power inhere in him, and prompt his murder, we suspect, at the hands of John Jasper, whose violence prompts his identification with the rebellious colonial subject. In him, it becomes most evident that the colonizing effort is one which is at least as much concerned to police the self as it is the colonies. From the outset, Jasper embodies specific fears of the colonial 'other', specifically the Oriental 'other', sharing as he does a bed in the opium den with a Chinaman and a Lascar, as well as the 'haggard woman' who runs the den (p. 37, ch. 1). In his intimacy with the other men, and in the intensity of his loving–hating relationship with Edwin, he also invokes an identification of the threat of the East with effeminacy and homosexuality. The whole novel is effectively a consideration of the effect of the colonial relationship upon the figure of the Englishman, the gentleman who ostensibly operates, and benefits from, the colonial enterprise. *Edwin Drood* demonstrates that such an enterprise is concerned at least as much with controlling the repressed 'other' which is inherent in English society as it is with controlling the otherness which is deemed colonial. Indeed, it shows how the need for colonization comes into being, as that which is considered other and extraneous to English masculinity is displaced onto the colonial subject.

In 1889, George Romanes would write, in an essay on 'Mental Evolution in Man':

> When we come to consider the case of the savages, and through them the case of prehistoric man, we shall find that, in the great interval which lies between such grades of mental evolution and our own, we are brought far on the way toward bridging the psychological distance which separates the gorilla from the gentleman.
>
> (Quoted in Brantlinger, *Rule of Darkness*, p. 186)

He thus encapsulated the need inherent in the anthropological, trading, military and religious practices which made up colonialism to reinforce the divide between civilization and the jungle, the gentleman and the savage who, Darwin had advised, was some way between gorilla and man. However, as we have seen, and as *The Mystery of Edwin Drood* makes perfectly clear, the increasingly brutal efforts needed to maintain the Empire brought the 'gentleman' ever nearer to acknowledging his participation in that savagery which he so deplored.

The properties of the gentleman

Such a recognition was in line with a more general reconfiguring of the gentleman in the 1860s. In a predominantly urban society, exhibiting the complexities engendered by Britain's industrial successes, the definition of the gentleman as one possessing land, and an income deriving from that land, no longer held good. Both at home and abroad, a new urban definition was needed, and was partly provided by the public schools, such as Rugby, which produced boys fit for the breed of bureaucrats needed for the home and colonial civil services. The nomination 'gentleman' rather helped to define the new breed of professional man who came about as a result of the reforms made to the Civil Service and the Church at this time. No longer the nepotistic preserve of the Tite Barnacles in *Little Dorrit*, the civil service instituted exams, and recruited on merit following the Northcote-Trevelyan *Report on the Organisation of the Permanent Civil Service* in 1854. As Robin Gilmour notes in *The Idea of the Gentleman in the Victorian Novel*, such reforms did not introduce a whole new breed of men into the service, but rather shifted the focus onto recruiting from the public schools rather than from the aristocracy.[28] These were not, of course, absolutely discrete groups, but, in the notional distinction between them made by recruitment examinations, a drive towards professionalism, and the creation of a new urban elite, was begun.

Trollope's *The Last Chronicle of Barset* (1866) demonstrates that elite in action in a novel which, based in the Cathedral close and rectories of Barsetshire, extends its interests into the legal offices of Silverbridge and London, and the private office of the Government minister Sir Raffle Buffle. However, its primary concern is to maintain the gentlemanliness of the Reverend Mr Crawley against the specific, and mistaken, criminal charge of theft, and to try to assert the absolute compatibility of the social accoutrements of the gentleman with the religious mission to care for parishioners' souls. It ends in asserting the resilience of the 'gentleman' as a form of identification which supersedes social standing, and the incompatibilities of social life. Through all his vicissitudes, his absolute poverty, Crawley remains a gentleman; indeed, this provides a defence almost as strong as does his profession against the accusation of theft. At the end of the novel, Crawley and the worldly, wealthy, landowning Archdeacon Grantly meet, as the fathers of children who are about to marry each other. Regretting his own poverty, Crawley wishes that he and Grantly met on more equal grounds, to which the Archdeacon, who has objected to the marriage throughout the novel, can now reply, 'We stand . . . on the only perfect level on which such men can meet each other. We are both gentlemen'.[29]

The novel has, however, a nostalgic feel to it, and a sometimes wistful quality when it comes to invoking the figure of the gentleman, and rightly so, for as Trollope would have been aware, since at least 1859, that title had been subject to a broader application which begins with Samuel Smiles's *Self-Help* (1859), in which the assurance is given that, by the right amount of diligent effort, a man might raise himself and his family up the social scale (a notion which sits awkwardly, even ironically, alongside Darwin's writing). Smiles's text is predicated upon the possibility of an individual being sufficiently able to control his own progress and fortune that, he can achieve the status of 'The True Gentleman', to which, according to the case-studies and inspiring tales of which his book is made up, any man might reasonably aspire. To be a true gentleman is rather a matter of character than of birth and possessions:

> Riches and rank have no necessary connection with genuine gentlemanly qualities. The poor man may be a true gentleman – in spirit and in daily life. He may be honest, truthful, upright, polite, temperate, courageous, self-respecting and self-helping – that is, be a true gentleman. The poor man with a rich spirit is in all ways superior to the rich man with a poor spirit.[30]

The concept of the gentleman in Smiles's developmental sense is an important one in fiction of the period. In *North and South*, the term is one of the grounds upon which Margaret Hale and Mr Thornton's dispute is carried out, and a negotiated compromise reached. He advocates the virtue of blunt good behaviour and morality, she of delicacy of feeling. In Smiles, and eventually in Thornton, the two are united. *Great Expectations* sees Pip working through an empty affectation of superficial gentlemanliness in the first enjoyment of his wealth, only to find a truer form of it in a relative poverty which is brightened by compassion, loyalty, and hard work. Pip and Thornton do, however, both belong to the ever-broadening middle class, and enjoy the benefits of education and some social standing. George Eliot's hero in *Adam Bede*, another text of 1859, is a more controversial figure, an artisan-gentleman.

Adam Bede is the first full-length novel written by Eliot, who had previously produced the three stories that make up *Scenes of Clerical Life* in 1857. In it, Adam Bede demonstrates the grounds of character by which he is enabled to move from his initial position as a carpenter in Jonathan Burge's yard to owning the yard himself, and being the head of his own household. Adam has moved up in the world, and yet the hierarchical structure of that world has not changed. Despite Adam's fight with him, and his moral weaknesses, Arthur Donnithorne remains the squire of the

village, and Adam his loyal friend. However, the centre of gravity has
changed. Moral worth now lies with Adam and his wife, the former
preacher Dinah Morris, and its tenets now are seen to be firmly embedded
within the sphere of work and home, rather than the halls of inherited
position. Despite its being set back at the turn of the century, the novel
nonetheless invokes the new characteristics of the middle classes of the
1850s in the grounds of Adam's rise to prosperity. It naturalizes their own
ascendance, and puts them firmly at the centre of English culture, and
Eliot's own readership.[31]

Adam Bede's setting in the past is typical of Eliot's work. All but one of
her novels (the exception being *Daniel Deronda*) are set in a very specifically
invoked past which not only enables the drawing of historical parallels, but
is crucial to her understanding of the individual. The possibility and composition of individuality was the prime concern of John Stuart Mill's *On
Liberty* (also 1859), where he espouses an understanding of the individual
profoundly at odds with that of Eliot. The declared object of Mill's essay is
'to assert one very simple principle', namely that:

> the sole end for which mankind are warranted, individually or
> collectively, in interfering with the liberty of action of any of their
> number, is self-protection. That the only purpose for which power can
> be rightfully exercised over any member of a civilised community,
> against his will, is to prevent harm to others. His own good, either
> physical or moral, is not a sufficient warrant.[32]

Mill was not primarily concerned here with the practice of governmental
laissez-faire, but rather with what he saw as the diminution of the possibility
of individuality within a society which seemed to him to be still in thrall to
an Anglicanism based on restraint and repression, and which subsequently
looked set to produce only abject conformity in its members. The individual
should rather be allowed to fulfil his or her gifts, and thus to produce a
various, divergent and ultimately stronger community. There is currently, he
writes, 'scarcely any outlet for energy in this country apart from business'
(p. 70).

Of particular concern to Mill is the effect on the individual of custom, the
'despotism' of which:

> is everywhere the standing hindrance to human advancement, being in
> unceasing antagonism to that disposition to aim at something better
> than customary, which is called, according to circumstances, the spirit
> of liberty, or that of progress or improvement.

(p. 70)

In this, Mill and Eliot are absolutely opposed. For her, custom is the lifeblood of community, the sharing of which confers identity, and a sustaining organicism which is at the heart of what it means to be human. In her essay 'The Natural History of German Life', Eliot notes the extent to which the German peasant is ruled by 'that dim instinct, that reverence for traditional custom', which is to him 'his supreme law'.[33] The energizing fissure in most of Eliot's novels is between an experience of individuality which demands present gratification and a more historical identification with family and community which would subdue the individual in the light of that community's needs. Nowhere is this schism more bitterly felt than in *The Mill on the Floss*, where Maggie has to choose between fulfilling her love for Stephen Guest or honouring her family. Significantly, she fleetingly succumbs to temptation when she surrenders to the moment when 'Memory was excluded' (p. 589, bk. 6, ch. 12). Eliot would fundamentally reject Mill's conception that the individual can be regarded as in any way distinct from his or her community: the two are ineluctably bound in an organic structure which is as sustaining as it may appear to be constricting.

Adam Bede exemplifies this relationship between the past, place, and person, stressing, as *The Origin of Species* would do later that year, the importance for nurture of environment. Adam is the product of Hayslope, and his tragedy is appropriately bound up in the life of the community, his resolution also worked through that community's pre-existing structure. The organic community is the ultimate goal and good within Eliot's work and morality, a morality which takes a form distinct from the socially motivated caricatures and strictures of Dickens. It is rather imbued with the earnestness of the evangelical faith which Eliot had been reared in, but for which she substitutes instead a humanist understanding of the universe, and the novelist as a didactic, substitute, religious guide. Her morality depends upon the extension to, and incorporation of, the reader within the community of the novel's sympathy and understanding. In 'The Natural History', she writes:

> The greatest benefit we owe to the artist, whether painter, poet, or novelist, is the extension of our sympathies. . . . Art is the nearest thing to life; it is a mode of amplifying experience and extending our contact with our fellow-men beyond the bounds of our personal lot.
>
> (p. 110)

The medium of this sympathy is the artist's minute attention to the representation of the 'real characteristics', the 'natural history' (p. 108) of a person or class, which can 'surprise' the reader into 'that attention to what is apart from themselves, which may be called the raw material of moral sentiment' (p. 110).

Eliot's aesthetic theory as expressed here, and in chapter 17 of *Adam Bede*, where she likens her prose to the 'rare, precious quality of truthfulness' of Dutch still-life paintings,[34] is an amalgamation of her knowledge of art history and the criticism of Ruskin, of her reading of Wordsworth, Scott and Dickens, her study of Auguste Comte's theories of organicism, and her pre-Darwinian appreciation of the operation of natural laws. As such the theory exemplifies, too, Eliot's aesthetic strategy of combining an extraordinary breadth of learning and references in her novels which, as we will see, act to extend the range and ramifications of her fiction as it is allowed to incorporate the implications and effects of the other arts and sciences to which she refers. What most concerns me here, however, is Eliot's insistence on truthfulness, and on the social responsibility of the novelist to be true. This responsibility manifests itself in ways absolutely distinct from Dickens's sense of outrage, and his deliberate crafting of an audience, both inside and outside his fiction, which will carry the moral responsibility of acting out the fundamental mechanisms of social cohesion. Eliot's is rather a voice which assumes with the mantle of novelist a responsibility to negotiate the troubling times besetting her readers. This meant, for instance, that in 1867 she was invited by her publisher John Blackwood to contribute an 'Address to Working Men' from Felix Holt to *Blackwood's Magazine*, which would enjoin upon working men a recognition of their new responsibilities under the second Reform Act. Ironically, of course, few working men would be in a position to read *Blackwood's Magazine*, so the reassuring voice of Felix, who preached a recognition of the mutual interdependency of the metaphorical body of society, would have been read rather by those middle classes who felt threatened by the Reform Act.

The second Reform Act was passed in 1867, following much political manoeuvring over the precise terms of enfranchisement and the partisan advantage to be gained by such nice calculations, and some public agitation in London in 1866 and 1867. Initially prompted by an evident discrepancy in constituency size,[35] the Act's changes to the franchise gained most public notice, though of course the two aspects operate hand in hand. At stake was the bestowal of public responsibility and determination, a right previously accorded to those landowners and members of the aristocracy having direct control over the lives of their tenants. However, just as the relationship between the idea of the gentleman and 'land' began to come adrift, so too now did that of the franchise and the gentleman. The roots of the concept of the stature conferred by land persisted in the property qualifications variously proposed as qualifications for suffrage, but they now pertained to rental and rating values for property, rather than land which was owned outright. The new franchise qualifications were considered with a mixture of minute statistical attention, last-minute desperation, and an overwhelming desire not to include too many of the working classes, and added 938,000 voters to an electorate of 1,056,000 in England and Wales. Though working-class voters predominated in the industrial towns, the redistribution of boundaries and seats acted to minimize their political effect.[36]

In introducing his bill in March 1867, Disraeli had referred to the 'manliness' of the household suffrage qualification (Hoppen, *The Mid-Victorian Generation*, p. 250), presumably as a form of safeguard against fears of cowardly insurrection. Here, it would seem that his 'manliness' might be understood as synonymous with that proposed by Mr Thornton, and thus as including a form of the gentlemanly which could be extended to the working classes. Such a form is represented in Felix Holt, set up by Eliot and Blackwood as the mediator of the new political developments. Of poor but respectable birth, Felix represents radicalism as a form of social democracy, of equity before God, and as a branch of politics uniquely untouched by worldly concerns. In the riots attending the Treby Magna elections, Felix finds himself caught up in acts of violence, and is eventually charged with the murder of a constable, while in fact trying to divert and control the mob. In this incident, and in the eventual revelation of the truth, as opposed to how the riot seemed to eyes prejudiced by fear, we may see the social urgency underlying Eliot's call for truth in art. Only by actively trying to discover truth can prejudice be broken down, and an organic society be substituted for one riven by distrust and class exclusivity. In his 'Address', Felix suggests that the responsible working man does indeed 'understand that a society, to be well off, must be made up chiefly of men who consider the general good as well as their own', and that:

> society stands before us like that wonderful piece of life, the human body, with all its various parts depending on one another, and with a terrible liability to get wrong because of that delicate dependence.[37]

Far from seeking to overthrow class distinctions, however, the working man appreciates that the greater necessity is to 'perform [his] particular work under the strong pressure of responsibility to the nation at large' (p. 491). This incorporation of the working man within the matrices of national responsibility is important in being addressed, however notionally, to that working figure himself. No longer simply one of a mass to be anonymously conscripted in a national effort, the working man is now, by right of the franchise, to be enjoined and self-consciously incorporated within the body politic.

That incorporation led directly to another piece of legislation which would have far-reaching effects for democracy, concepts of citizenship, and the novel. It was felt that the new generation of voters enfranchised in 1867 needed to be educated to take their place in the political arena. As Jane Garnett writes, 'education for citizenship required not just the three Rs, but the cultivation of a critical and flexible intellect'.[38] Politicians were also motivated by what were seen as the international competitive advantages of a literate work-force, and by the example of the educated Prussian army in the Franco-Prussian war of 1870. The Education Act of 1870 thus sought to provide elementary education for all children aged between 5 and 13, and instituted local school boards (of which women might be members) to monitor attendance and the conditions of the new schools. In 1870 around half of the children in the country were registered as attending schools which had been inspected. Others had no schooling, or attended institutions which were probably inadequate. By 1873, 2.2 million children were on the registers of government-aided schools, around 74 per cent of those eligible to attend.[39] Such an Act was at least as effective a form of enfranchisement as the Reform Act of 1867.

At various points in this chapter, we have seen how important property was perceived as being, both in political and personal terms. In the latter years of this period, two parliamentary Acts further eroded the connection between gentlemen and property, and the rights and attributes involved in that conjunction. In 1870 the first Irish Land Act was passed, which ostensibly increased the rights of tenants, and the security of those occupying land without a lease, but which left plenty of loop-holes for landlords. Most importantly, however, as the Cambridge historian J.R. Seeley pointed out in a *Macmillan's Magazine* article of that year, 'that great monopoly which the age ... steadfastly maintains ... the right of private property itself' had been con-travened.[40] Also in that year, the first Married Women's Property Act was passed. Up until that point, a woman had no automatic right to maintain ownership of property which was hers before marriage, nor to possess her own savings and earnings after marriage. As we can see in *The Woman in White*, when Laura Fairlie's marriage settlement is being discussed, a family might protect a woman's position in her marriage contract, but that was her only legal safeguard against the kind of unscrupulous draining of her finan-cial resources to which Betsey Trotwood falls victim in *David Copperfield*. The Act was disappointing to its supporters, in that it applied only to women's right to own property which had come into her possession since her marriage. However, the Act did begin to unlock the age-old assumption, and legal prac-tice, of coverture, that is, a wife's absorption into the being of her husband, whereby she had no right to any form of independent legal standing. As coverture was challenged, so too were the terms of contemporary marriage, and along with them the cultural, sexual, and political identities of men and women. As the century progressed, the ramifications of such reconfigurations of the markers of identity began to be felt in both international and domestic political arenas. And, as ever greater numbers of the population achieved literacy, the novel was ever more fully brought into those arenas too.

Notes

1 Charles Darwin, *The Origin of Species* (Harmondsworth, 1985), p. 129.
2 Gillian Beer, *Darwin's Plots: Evolutionary Narrative in Darwin, George Eliot and Nineteenth-Century Fiction* (London, 1985), p. 7.
3 Trollope wrote six Barsetshire novels between 1855 and 1867, including *The Warden* (1855) and *Barchester Towers* (1857). Oliphant wrote her 'Chronicles of Carlingford' between 1863 and 1876, the best-known of the five novels being *Salem Chapel* (1863) and *Miss Marjoribanks* (1866).
4 Sally Shuttleworth, *George Eliot and Nineteenth-Century Science* (Cambridge, 1984), p. 53.
5 George Eliot, *The Mill on the Floss* (Harmondsworth, 1985), p. 656, conclusion.
6 Quoted in Robin Gilmour, *The Victorian Period: The Intellectual and Cultural Context of English Literature, 1830–1890*, p. 129.
7 Wilkie Collins, *The Law and the Lady* (Harmondsworth, 1998), pp. 299–300, ch. 39.
8 As Gilmour notes, Herbert Spencer was of a different opinion, seeing the move from homogeneity to heterogeneity within species as one of progress (*The Victorian Period*, p. 129).
9 Francis Power Cobbe, 'Fallacies of Memory' (1867), quoted in Cathy Tingle, 'Symptomatic Writings: Prefigurations of Freudian Theories and Models of the Mind in the Fiction of Sheridan Le Fanu, Wilkie Collins and George Eliot', unpub. doctoral dissertation (Leeds, 2000), p. 146.
10 Frances Power Cobbe, 'The Fallacies of Memory' (1867); quoted in Jenny Bourne Taylor and Sally Shuttleworth, eds, *Embodied Selves: An Anthology of Psychological Texts, 1830–1890*, pp. 150–4 (p. 151).
11 Henry James's 1865 review of Braddon's *Aurora Floyd* (1863), quoted in Lyn Pykett, *The Sensation Novel* (London, 1994), p. 6.
12 Henry James, 'The London Theaters', *Scribner's Monthly*, 21 (1880–81), 354–69 (p. 363).
13 Wilkie Collins, *No Name* (Harmondsworth, 1994), p. 191, Captain Wragge's chronicle for October 1846.
14 Mary E. Braddon, *Lady Audley's Secret* (London, 1985), p. 5, ch. 1.
15 *Mrs Beeton's Book of Household Management* (Oxford, 2000), p. 29.
16 29 per cent of army hospital admissions and 12.5 per cent of navy admissions in 1862 were for sexually transmitted diseases (Philippa Levine, *Victorian Feminism 1850–1900* (London, 1987), p. 145).
17 Michel Foucault, *The History of Sexuality: An Introduction* (Harmondsworth, 1978), p. 35.
18 Eliza Lynn Linton, 'The Girl of the Period', *Saturday Review*, 25 (1868), 339–49 (p. 339).

19 John Ruskin, 'Of Queen's Gardens', in *Sesame and Lilies* (London, 1911), p. 107.
20 Thomas Hughes, *Tom Brown's Schooldays* (Oxford, 1999), pp. 1–2.
21 Patrick Brantlinger, *Rule of Darkness: British Literature and Imperialism, 1830–1914* (Ithaca and London, 1988), p. 173.
22 Information about the Mutiny is taken from Bernard Porter, *The Lion's Share: A Short History of British Imperialism, 1850–1995* (London, 1996), pp. 29–48; Brantlinger, *Rule of Darkness*, pp. 199–222; and K. Theodore Hoppen, *The Mid-Victorian Generation 1846–1886* (Oxford, 1998), pp. 183–97.
23 For an account of the Jamaica Crisis, see Ronald Hyam, *Britain's Imperial Century, 1815–1914: A Study of Empire and Expansion* (Macmillan, 1993), pp. 151–4.
24 Suvendrini Perera, *Reaches of Empire: The English Novel from Edgeworth to Dickens* (New York, 1991), p. 116.
25 Porter gives figures for Indian exports to Britain in 1876: raw cotton £13.3 m., opium £11.1 m., rice, wheat and grains £6.4 m., oil seeds £5.5 m., hides £2.9 m., indigo £2.9 m., jute £2.8 m., tea £2.2 m., and manufactured cotton goods £2 m. (Porter, *The Lion's Share*, pp. 42–43).
26 Charles Dickens, *The Mystery of Edwin Drood* (Harmondsworth, 1974), p. 53, ch. 3.
27 That the novel is actually set somewhat earlier is suggested by Dickens's statement that the railway had not yet reached Cloisterham (p. 83, ch. 6), leading some critics to posit the 1840s as the period's setting. The novel being written and read in 1870, shortly after the opening of the Suez Canal, thus gives greater weight to its mention of engineering in Egypt.
28 Robin Gilmour, *The Idea of the Gentleman in the Victorian Novel* (London, 1981), pp. 92ff.
29 Anthony Trollope, *The Last Chronicle of Barset* (Oxford, 2001), p. 885, ch. 83.
30 Samuel Smiles, *Self-Help* (Harmondsworth, 1986), p. 240.
31 In 'Dinah's Blush, Maggie's Arm: Class, Gender and Sexuality in George Eliot's Early Novels', Margaret Homans argues that Eliot 'naturalizes middle-class values' by projecting them backwards 'onto rural 1807' (*Victorian Studies*, 36 (1993), 155–78 (pp. 164, 169)).
32 John Stuart Mill, *On Liberty, and Other Writings*, ed. by Stefan Collini (Cambridge, 1989), p. 13.
33 'The Natural History of German Life' (1856), in George Eliot, *Selected Essays, Poems and Other Writings* (Harmondsworth, 1990), pp. 107–39 (pp. 121, 126). The essay reviews two books on the German peasantry by Wilhelm Heinrich von Riehl.
34 George Eliot, *Adam Bede* (Harmondsworth, 1985), p. 223.
35 Hoppen gives the following examples of unevenness in representation:

> Honiton, Totnes, Wells, Marlborough, and Knaresborough together contained fewer than 23,000 people but returned as many members as the 1.5 million inhabitants of Liverpool, Manchester, Birmingham, Sheffield, and Leeds. The 334 English and Welsh borough members each 'represented' 26,000 people, the 162 county members no less than 70,000 each.
> (Hoppen, *The Mid-Victorian Generation*, p. 246)

36 The franchise was extended to include householders in the boroughs, lodgers in premises worth £10 a year, and county householders paying at least £12 in rates. All qualifications were subject to a residence requirement of one year, which kept large numbers off the register (Hoppen, *The Mid-Victorian Generation*, p. 253).

37 George Eliot, 'Address to Working Men, by Felix Holt', in *Felix Holt*, pp. 485–99 (p. 489).

38 Jane Garnett, 'Religious and Intellectual Life', in C. Matthew, ed., *The Nineteenth Century, 1815–1901* (Oxford, 2000), pp. 195–227 (p. 212).

39 Statistics are taken from Alec Ellis, *Educating Our Masters: Influences on the Growth of Literacy in Victorian Working-class Children* (Aldershot, 1985), p. 27.

40 J.R. Seeley, 'The English Revolution of the Nineteenth Century III', quoted in Hoppen, *The Mid-Victorian Generation*, p. 597.

|3|

1871–1885
Democracy and its discontents

With the death of Dickens in 1870, a unifying figure was lost to British fiction and culture. That Shakespearean quality which embraces all classes both within, and as an audience for, the work of fiction, was not to be seen again in the century. The fiction of 1871–85 investigates this loss of a sense of a national audience at a time when the concept of nation itself was experienced as a troublingly fragmented one. It was a time when Victoria was declared Empress of India by Disraeli (in 1876), but also when Ireland began to agitate forcibly for Home Rule, and when British interests in Africa were sufficiently troubled by European competitors that a full-scale 'Scramble' for the continent ensued. The inauguration of international football and cricket matches in Britain in 1872 and 1880 respectively perhaps provided a welcome opportunity for the celebration of national identity, but again it was an identity predicated upon competition.[1] At home, industrial productivity increased, but relatively declined against the newly competitive work-forces of Germany and America. The founding of the Society for the Protection of Ancient Buildings in 1877 and the Ancient Monuments Protection Act in 1882 suggest indeed that it was perhaps a time in which the nation self-consciously looked for stability of identity in the past rather than in the present or future.

The way we lived then

The late 1860s and early 1870s produced a number of novels which looked back to the late 1820s and early 1830s. *Felix Holt*, Trollope's *Phineas Finn* (1867–69) and George Eliot's *Middlemarch* all revert to that period, and in particular to the first Reform Act. In many respects, these novels seem to be positing the earlier time as that in which their own society is founded, suggesting in fact that it sees the beginnings of what was increasingly becoming known in the 1870s as the Victorian period, and of a number of narratives and concerns which would go on to define the rest of the century.

That earlier world is evoked for her late-1860s' audience by George Eliot in her introduction to *Felix Holt*:

> Five-and-thirty years ago the glory had not yet departed from the old coach-roads: the great roadside inns were still brilliant with well-polished tankards, the smiling glances of pretty barmaids, and the repartees of jocose ostlers; the mail still announced itself by the merry notes of the horn; the hedge-cutter or the rick-thatcher might still know the exact hour by the unfailing yet otherwise meteoric apparition of the pea-green Tally-ho or the yellow Independent; and elderly gentlemen in pony-chaises, quartering nervously to make way for the rolling swinging swiftness, had not ceased to remark that times were finely changed since they used to see the pack-horses and hear the tinkling of their bells on this very highway.

(p. 3)

This nostalgic evocation of bygone times signals the importance of the transport revolution in defining both the period in which the novel is set and that in which it is written. On transport depends communication, labour, markets, and, as the passage hints, even time. Until the growth of a national railway network, no need for a nationally agreed 'timetable' existed. Clearly the revolution in transport and speed inaugurated by the railways from 1825 onwards had come to seem a defining characteristic of the earlier part of the century. As Thackeray writes in 1860: 'We who have lived before railways were made, belong to another world.'[2]

In *Middlemarch* the coming of the railway causes great consternation, fears that cows will cast their calves, and that the plight of the poor will somehow be made worse by their advent, but the railways are defended by Caleb Garth as a necessity, and as ultimately 'a good thing'.[3] For the readers of *Felix Holt* and *Middlemarch*, the knowledge of the imminent changes about to befall the nation would underlie this evocation of the past about to fall victim to the railway age. But the *Felix Holt* passage itself, in its recognition of the 'elderly gentlemen', is already cognisant of the perpetual impetus to change, the always already obsolete and superseded quality that even the fondest act of nostalgia confers. That double vision is crucial to reading Eliot, and to assessing her relationship with her own time, a relationship which she posits and complicates far more self-consciously and deliberately than any of her contemporaries.

The earlier period was also, of course, the time of 'pocket boroughs, a Birmingham unrepresented in Parliament and compelled to make strong representations out of it' (*Felix Holt*, p. 3, introduction). These are the days before the passing of the Reform Act of 1832 which did so much to change electoral processes in Britain. Ambiguous and still debated in its effects, the Act nonetheless incontrovertibly initiated an impulse towards democracy which touched upon other areas than the purely parliamentary, and which is arguably one of the defining characteristics of the Victorian period. One might argue that the railways, which for the first time made possible the mass movement of large numbers of people, were similarly part of a movement towards an effective democratization of opportunity, as were education reforms which effected the most significant enfranchisement through literacy. These various manifestations of democracy all contributed to the more fragmented sense of the nation which pervades society, politics, and the novel after 1870. Rather than melding the nation into a coherent whole, the move towards democracy within a burgeoning commodity culture created a diversity of markets and constituencies. It is perhaps her apprehension of such a fragmentation which prompted Eliot's best developed vision of the fundamental organicism of society in *Middlemarch*, but she is also clearly inspired by the advent of the second Reform Act, and by the need to persist in investigating the possibilities for reform in an ever-evolving society.

For the critic Sidney Colvin, the dissonance between the two periods conditions the writing of the novel: 'To the old world belong the elements of her experience, to the new world the elements of her reflection on experience'.[4] The two epochs, to borrow Colvin's phrase, are linked through the issue of reform, which is shown to be a determining phenomenon of more than just the political sphere. In *Middlemarch*, Will Ladislaw and Mr Brooke's efforts for electoral reform are read alongside Lydgate's attempts to reform medical research and diagnosis, alongside Caleb Garth and later Fred Vincy's improvements in agricultural practices, alongside Eliot's own analysis of developments in Biblical scholarship, and alongside the various ways in which the novel's women perceive and attempt to subvert the restrictions of their position. In all of these arenas, changes had been made since 1830, but much still remained to be done. For instance, medical practice had been transformed in particular by the use of chloroform (first used as general anaesthetic in 1847, and taken by Queen Victoria during the birth of Prince Leopold in 1853), and by the development of an antiseptic method of surgery by Lister in 1867. Regulation and professionalization began to inform this, as well as other careers, with the founding of the British Medical Association (BMA) in 1854. On-going public health and sanitary reforms also further improved the health of the nation. But in the years immediately following *Middlemarch*, and in the wake of the pioneering examples of Elizabeth Blackwell and Elizabeth Garrett, a London School of Medicine for Women was set up (in 1874), and in 1875 women were allowed to sit surgeons' exams and Elizabeth Garrett was admitted to the BMA.

Within *Middlemarch*, however, Dorothea's ambitions to serve, to be publicly useful, are thwarted. Critics including Colvin and R.H. Hutton strongly resented Eliot's suggestion that society was in some measure responsible for Dorothea's being buried in marriage. (Their reactions are of course instructive in suggesting how far women still had to go to enjoy the full range of opportunities enjoyed by men.) Rather than being able to find an appropriate forum for her desire to do good, Dorothea lacks the opportunity for the fulfilment of a vocation. The novel's profoundest celebration is of the experience of vocation, be it Lydgate's thwarted and fleeting thirst for medical research which dawns upon him in the memorable scene in his uncle's library (ch. 15), or Caleb Garth's life of active service, in which he aspires to the noblest ambition of:

> getting a bit of the country into good fettle, as they say, and putting men into the right way with their farming, and getting a bit of good contriving and solid building done – that those who are living and those who come after will be the better for it. I'd sooner have it than a fortune. I hold it the most honourable work there is.
>
> (p. 403, ch. 40)

Incidentally, this celebration of vocation gives an interesting gloss on Eliot's relationship to a period of national prosperity and relative ease. Lest the nation forget itself she advocates, Ruskin-like, a relationship with the site of work, and with the human meaning of work, most viscerally represented by Lydgate's enquiries, which will guard against the temptations besetting Bulstrode, the Evangelical banker, who in his own more tortuously self-knowing way is as great a swindler as *Little Dorrit*'s Mr Merdle or Trollope's Augustus Melmotte.

There is, however, a difficulty when it comes to assessing the possibilities for vocation open to women, in both the 1830s and, the novel seems to imply, the 1870s. Dorothea's own highly developed sense of vocation finds its only possible outlet or tributary in the uncertain opportunities of marriage. Dorothea's early vigour and resolution to help her uncle's tenants is swallowed up in her first marriage, which seems initially to provide an alternative outlet for vocation in her services to Casaubon and his scholarship, but which ends by trapping her energies within the dark labyrinth of his egotism and the studies which already lag far behind those of his German contemporaries. Sexually, too, the marriage is thwarted, and, Eliot implies, is unlikely to have been consummated. Even her second, much more joyful marriage to Will Ladislaw only provides her with a vicarious life of service as the wife of an 'ardent public man' (pp. 836, finale). Some felt it:

> a pity that so substantive and rare a creature should have been absorbed into the life of another, and be only known in a certain circle as a wife and mother. But no one stated exactly what else that was in her power she ought rather to have done.
>
> (p. 836)

Eliot goes on to warn that, as 'there is no creature whose inward being is so strong that it is not greatly determined by what lies outside it', her readers must beware, as they are daily 'preparing the lives of many Dorotheas' (p. 838). There could not be a clearer warning that conditions for women had not yet changed sufficiently since the 1830s. Virtue and marriage are no longer their own rewards in a society gradually and democratically opening up opportunities to more of its members.

Middlemarch was being written and published on the cusp of change, in which the example of Dorothea was highly evocative for those readers and friends of Eliot, such as Bessie Rayner Parkes and Barbara Bodichon, who were variously involved in developments in women's education and in early suffrage agitation. Bodichon was one of the earliest readers to give voice to her sense of doom as she saw Dorothea's relationship with Casaubon unfold. She wrote to Eliot that reading the early parts of the novel was like watching 'a child dancing into a quick sand on a summer morning'.[5] Though Eliot herself was wary of being too publicly involved in the early women's movement, there is no doubt that the effect of her writings was to galvanize these women's efforts. As we have seen already, women made great strides forward in the medical profession in the 1870s, and in 1872 and 1875 respectively were able to take places at Girton and Newnham colleges in Cambridge. Though not reading for degrees, they attended lectures and in 1881 were able to sit Honours exams. Greater employment opportunities for middle-class women followed which made marriage only one of a number of available life-choices.

Even when Eliot was writing, however, there were women, such as Josephine Butler, who headed both families and important national campaigning organizations, and who indeed performed those 'ardent deeds', the medium for which Eliot believed had vanished forever. So why did Eliot not recognize such achievements? Interestingly, those critics who were offended by Eliot's criticism of society's restrictions on women failed to argue from the evidence of high-achieving women in their society, perhaps thus unconsciously supporting Eliot's critique. Gillian Beer has argued persuasively that 'George Eliot early recognised that the exceptional changes nothing. . . . It carried with it no transformation of the ordinary',[6] and indeed perhaps might have seemed to militate against the celebration of the organic society within Eliot's work.

But it is also the case that the activating context of Eliot's writing is not just the immediate present, or a carefully selected moment in the not too distant past, but rather the centuries represented by the quotations, allusions, and epigrams within the text. Though carefully historically situated ('When George the Fourth was still reigning over the privacies of Windsor, when the Duke of Wellington was Prime Minister, and Mr Vincy was mayor of the old corporation in Middlemarch' (p. 188, ch. 19)), the consummately provincial life with which Eliot is concerned reverberates within a dense web of allusion, just one part of which links Dorothea to Ariadne and Will to Apollo, Rosamond to the Sirens, and Lydgate to a doomed Odysseus. Such allusions are themselves of course a profoundly determining context. They tell us much of what the Victorian novelist felt she could expect of her readers, both in terms of their knowledge and commitment to her novel, and how Eliot herself felt her own present to be historically and dynamically situated. The past is continuous with the present, its echoes sounding out contemporary themes. Henry James might have felt the novel to be painfully of the present in its, for him, discordant learning and language in which he heard 'too often an echo of Messrs. Darwin and Huxley',[7] but their voices were just two among the many from the various historical epochs which inform Eliot's text, and which problematize the novelist's consideration of how her characters can live in the present. In *Middlemarch*, the notion of a determining context is one informed by her voluminous reading and by an intellectual inquiry and generosity unmatched by any other Victorian English novelist.

The way we live now

The same could of course be said of Eliot's *Daniel Deronda*, a novel even more densely allusive in its substance. That later text is also Eliot's only really contemporary fiction, and a full-blown 'condition of England' novel, but one which finds its solution in its wealth of allusion. It appeared in eight monthly parts in 1876, shortly after Trollope's *The Way We Live Now*, which was also concerned, as its title suggests, with the state of the nation. In the early to mid-1870s, and particularly after 1873, that nation was one perceiving itself to be, if not in a state of decline, at least lacking in the optimism earlier associated with its burgeoning industrial status. The nation identified by the two novelists is one defined rather by the commercial exploitation of a second wave of industrialism, and by the extent to which such financial concerns infiltrate and determine every level and aspect of English society. Though absolutely distinct in their conclusions, and in their treatment of Jewish characters, the two novelists concur exactly in their use of gambling as the defining activity and energizing motif in their texts.

Historians differ as to whether or not British industry did begin to show signs of absolute decline in the early 1870s. It may rather be the case, as Hoppen argues, that the 'coincidence of increasing industrial maturity, rapid advances by rivals abroad, and spasmodic bad times in the years after 1873' combined to create that impression.[8] As its rivals, notably Germany and America, were developing new industries with new stock and equipment, Britain was faced with the prospect of making do with existing systems, or upgrading. The economic reasons for the latter were often not immediately pressing, and so old practices often prevailed. This resulted in the relative decline of British growth rates when compared with those of Germany and America. Furthermore, Britain's share of the world market in manufactured exports fell from 45 to 29 per cent between 1872 and 1899, with Germany's rising from 12 to 21 per cent.[9] Investors then turned to overseas markets for their financial speculations, and found opportunities particularly in America for reaping huge dividends. The railway boom came late to the States, occurring in the 1860s and 1870s, during which decades the miles of track more than trebled from 30,800 in 1860 to 94,200 in 1880.[10] This development, along with the new availability of refrigerated freight systems, would come to have a devastating effect on British agriculture later in the century, and emphasizes the extent to which, at this period, Britain found itself often uncomfortably having to take account of its place in a global market in which it was not necessarily the senior partner, and in which the securities of the Empire had begun to give way.

Historically then, as well as in terms of the subject-matter of fiction, attention in Britain was turned to speculative rather than manufacturing opportunities, a development in part also facilitated by the growth of limited companies following the passing of the Companies Act of 1862. Originally intended simply to limit liabilities in the event of business failures, it seems also to have had the effect, as Ensor puts it, of 'divorcing the ownership from the management of factories and works' (*England, 1870–1914*, p. 112), and hence of destroying once and for all the last vestiges of what writers such as Gaskell had seen as the redeeming factor of patriarchalism in the manufacturing sector. Men such as John Thornton, the 'owner-entrepreneurs', who live among their workers, are replaced by the anonymous figures of the shareholders, whose concern is rather for their dividends than for workers. Control was devolved on behalf of the shareholders to boards of directors, 'often representing only financial, social, or personal "pulls" and devoid of any specialized understanding of the firm or even of the industry' (Ensor, *England, 1870–1914*, p. 113).

Such is the state of things that Trollope exploits in *The Way We Live Now*, a novel firmly embedded in the most up-to-the-minute concerns of the nation. The South Central Pacific and Mexican Railway epitomizes the type of financial opportunity being successfully exploited in contemporary Britain, and yet Trollope represents it as an almost entirely fraudulent concern, placing at its head in England the supposedly fabulously wealthy, but also probably criminal, Augustus Melmotte. Little is known of his antecedents, though it is suspected that he may be Jewish, and he was by his own private confession born into poverty, with no knowledge of his parents. He comes to England in the wake of commercial collapses in Paris and Vienna (which have their historical counterpart in the European financial crisis which began in Vienna in 1873), and out of which Melmotte did very well. He is a compound of several confidence tricksters well known to the public of the 1870s. Like Dickens's Merdle, he recalls the MP John Sadleir who committed suicide in 1856 to escape prosecution for a series of frauds estimated to be worth around a million pounds. Like Melmotte, he forged property documents and was involved in defrauding a railway company (in his case, the Royal Swedish Railway Company). Trollope was not, however, lacking in more contemporary figures to inspire his Melmotte, as John Sutherland shows in his introduction to the Oxford World's Classics edition. Indeed, so concerned was parliament at this time with the possible abuse of international financial agreements that it set up a select committee to investigate loans (including that made for the Interoceanic Railway in Honduras) with foreign states. This was in operation as Trollope was writing, and its report came out simultaneously with the volume issue of the novel in July 1875.[11]

The novel is, then, very much about Trollope's 'now', and how he sees the figure of Melmotte as endemic of the way his society lives. Melmotte is essentially a gambler who trades on people's gullibility and their own desire for the possibility of great (and preferably unearned) wealth in order to part them with the money and property that they do have. Trollope shows such a desire for easy wealth permeating the marriage market too, where Lady Carbury, on behalf of her son, and Georgiana Longestaffe work through the financial and social permutations of their marital possibilities. The secret ballot, introduced in 1872, and reviled by Trollope as somehow underhand, also comes to seem like a form of irresponsible gambling for which one is not publicly answerable, and by which means a man like Melmotte, who appeals to selfish interests, can be elected. The young aristocrats at the Beargarden who spend most of their waking hours gambling at the card tables are clearly only the most visible aspect of a world given over to speculation.

Trollope's antidote to these men is Roger Carbury, the squire of Carbury Manor, who is distinguished by a lack of worldly self-interest, by his untiring devotion to Hetta Carbury, and by a code of morals which prevents his taking anything like an unfair advantage of Paul Montague, his rival for Hetta's hand. Such virtues lead Roger to seem old before his time, but are not his primary distinguishing feature for Trollope. Rather, that lies in his attachment to his land and his parish. The new commercial opportunities were absolutely divorced from local considerations, spanning as they did many thousands of miles, and uniting people in a new democracy of financial opportunity. Trollope seems to regard this cutting free from local responsibilities as profoundly morally disabling. Roger lives on his own land, among his own people, to whom he is a benevolent patriarch, and from whom he exacts respect and obedience. Land is the guarantee of the terms of their relationship. That the Longestaffes sell their house, Pickering, to Melmotte is an indication of how far commerce corrupts the relationship between land and morality, and is of course the speculation which triggers Melmotte's downfall.

Before it collapses into a disappointingly traditional series of redeeming marriages, and dispatches its miscreants and misfits abroad, the novel is a pungent exposition of the terms of contemporary wealth and influence. However, it is not without its own prejudices and difficulties for a later reader. The sexual double standard is exposed, but left largely unchallenged; domestic violence is reviled but treated as endemic, and the novel is deeply anti-semitic. Though allowing the Jewish banker Brehgert a nobility beyond his society's expectations, and contrary to the slurs heaped upon him, the novel nonetheless is freely spoken in its derogatory suspicions as to Melmotte's Jewishness, and invokes the figure of the then Prime Minister, Disraeli, son of a convert from Judaism, with some distaste. Traditionally associated with finance, pawnbroking, and speculation, the figure of the Jew risks being scapegoated in a novel which had seemed bravely to seek to expose the iniquities of contemporary Britain, but which ends rather in a retreat from the dilemmas Melmotte's presence had invoked.

In contrast George Eliot's final novel *Daniel Deronda*, the most ambitious and challenging English novel of the century, engages with the same themes as Trollope, but rather sees in the Jewish race a solution to the shortcomings of English society of the time. This novel, too, takes gambling as its primary *modus vivendi*, and is inspired by Eliot seeing a young woman engrossed in play at the Kursaal in Hamburg in 1872. She wrote of the scene to John Blackwood:

> The Kursaal is to me a hell, not only for the gambling but for the light and heat of the gas, and we have seen enough of its monstrous hideousness. There is very little dramatic *Stoff* to be picked up by watching or listening. The saddest thing to be witnessed is the play of Miss Leigh, Byron's grand niece, who is only 26 years old, and is completely in the grasp of this mean, money-making demon. It made me cry to see her young fresh face among the hags and brutally stupid men around her.
>
> (Letter of 4 October 1872; in *The George Eliot Letters*, 5, 314)

Contrary to her thoughts at the time, this moment provides a wonderfully dramatic opening to her novel, and encapsulates the themes of the text to follow. Gwendolen Harleth is trapped within an economy of gambling which eventually entails her staking her own being in a marriage based entirely on monetary want. In this, as in the casino, she is observed by Daniel Deronda, the ward of an English baronet, who is later proven to be Jewish, and who provides Gwendolen with the only possibility of redemption from the corrupt English society in which she is entrapped.

It is a society degraded in every respect and at every level, and it demonstrates its corruption primarily in the poverty of its cultural life. Gwendolen's choice of the music that she will sing at an evening party reveals both her and her audience, in the words of the German composer Klesmer, as preferring 'a dandling, canting see-saw kind of [music] – the passion and thought of people without any breadth of horizon'.[12] Invited to sing something 'larger', Gwendolen retreats 'with a sinking of heart at the sudden width of horizon opened around her small musical performance'. Such moral agoraphobia characterizes both Gwendolen and her English context. In an elaborate descriptive metaphor, Eliot constructs a series of images of her main characters based on references to painters which confirms her English characters' inwardness. While they are represented according to the allegorical, aristocratic style of Reynolds and Van Dyck, the Jewish characters are described in terms of continental art, of Rembrandt's rabbis, and in particular of Venetian painting. The link with Italy is instructive: the country had recently achieved unification, as Deronda hopes a Jewish state might also do. Perhaps Eliot is implying that England too might be re-made. But, most importantly, Hugh Witemeyer suggests, 'the Venetian school is appropriate to the Jewish characters in *Daniel Deronda*, who have preserved a vital contact with their ancient religion; whereas the modern school is appropriate to the English characters, who are vain and worldly'.[13]

Gwendolen's most significant cultural ambition is her desire to go on the stage, partly in order to avoid having to undertake her marriage to Grandcourt, a man wealthy, but wasted by years of debauchery, and partly to avoid the mundane calling of the governess, which was her only other viable economic alternative. Gwendolen is confident in her prospects of success, because she thinks that she would look well on stage, 'since she was more beautiful than [Rachel]', the leading actress of the day, described by Gwendolen as 'that thin Jewess' (p. 54, ch. 6). In her desire to act, Gwendolen stakes all on the moment of spectacle, on the impact of her looks, ignoring the years of dedicated study necessary before appearing on a stage, and the demands of vocation felt by performers. In this ambition, and in the rest of her life, Gwendolen denies history, substituting the imperatives of the moment for longer narratives of deserving. Such is the essence of gambling, and such desires similarly motivate Melmotte and the members of the Beargarden.

Opposed to these impulses in Eliot's novel is the example presented by her exalted Jewish characters, Daniel himself, Ezra Cohen, and his sister Mirah, all of whom live in a world determined by the historical narratives of Jewish teaching and suffering, and who see their lives taking part in a context of much greater dimensions than the merely contemporary. Mirah, for instance, holds herself to be rather a vessel for the transmission of music than the performer that Gwendolen desires to be. Crucially, too, these three live in a context which is European, if not worldwide, rather than simply British. Culturally, politically, as well as in religious terms, their outlooks exceed the degradations which Eliot describes as typically British at this time. This novel, too, ends with a marriage, but Daniel's and Mirah's wedding trip represents a permanent removal which they hope will result in a new Jewish state. Gwendolen remains a young widow, a figure troubling in her aspirations for a new life, and stymied by her context and her own weaknesses in her attempts to achieve it. As Gwendolen's and Daniel's farewell scene shows, the Jewish example can only teach perseverance and sustained effort across the years:

> Sobs rose, and great tears fell fast. Deronda would not let her hands go – held them still with one of his, and himself pressed her handkerchief against her eyes. She submitted like a half-soothed child, making an effort to speak, which was hindered by struggling sobs. At last she succeeded in saying brokenly –
>
> 'I said ... I said ... it should be better ... better with me ... for having known you.'

His eyes too were larger with tears. She wrested one of her hands from his, and returned his action, pressing his tears away.

'We shall not be quite parted,' he said. 'I will write to you always, when I can, and you will answer?'

He waited till she said in a whisper, 'I will try.'

'I shall be more with you than I used to be,' Daniel said with gentle urgency [. . .] 'Now we can perhaps never see each other again. But our minds may get nearer.'

(pp. 805–6, ch. 69)

Both *The Way We Live Now* and especially *Daniel Deronda* set England within a new world-order. The Empire is no longer the cushioning force that it once was, as England has to negotiate with and sometimes to be bested by its neighbours. These novels represent a sea-change in the way in which global relations are pictured, with England humbling itself as just one more player in the international market. At home too, however, images of the nation were ineluctably shifting. Though the country had been primarily urban for some time, agriculture still employed a larger number of workers than any other industry, and England relied heavily, both for produce and for a sense of national stability, upon the land. Yet now even that certainty was being challenged. The expansion of the American railways, combined with an abundance of cheap ocean transport, and the development of revolutionary new agricultural equipment with which to exploit more fully the great prairies, sent the price of imported wheat plummeting during the 1870s and early 1880s. These conditions combined with bad harvests (from 1875 to 1879) to bring misery to English villages, and to bankrupt even farmers of long standing. It is of course during these years that Thomas Hardy begins his series of pastoral novels, which, far from exalting the countryside, rather show it as appropriately riven by the same pressures for profit that mark the urban landscape, and its inhabitants as subject to the same temptations as experienced by town-dwellers.

Far From the Madding Crowd (1874) shows the destructive effects on the countryside of the intrusion of the gambler Sergeant Troy and of Bathsheba Everdene, whose need for conquest, or perhaps rather whose enthralment to the romantic intrigues deemed appropriate to young women of the time, brings chaos to her community. Bathsheba is just one of the fictional women of this period in whose story we see the elements of the sensation novel emerging into mainstream fiction. The stories of Bathsheba, Troy, and Boldwood are played out against a social and architectural tapestry of rustic life which, Hardy suggests, has remained unchanged for centuries. His warmest appreciation is bestowed on the shearing barn:

One could say about this barn, what could hardly be said of either the church or the castle, akin to it in age and style, that the purpose which had dictated its original erection was the same with that to which it was still applied ... the old barn embodied practices which had suffered no mutilation at the hands of time. Here at least the spirit of the ancient builders was at one with the spirit of the modern beholder.[14]

The building generates 'a feeling almost of gratitude, and quite of pride, at the permanence of the idea which had heaped it up' (p. 195). And yet, around the barn, and the traditional practices, change pushes on. Fanny Robins dying in the Casterbridge workhouse is a reminder of the poverty that now dogs agricultural life. In Gabriel Oak, too, one finds a man unlike his farming fathers, a man who reads, and works with equal authority alongside Boldwood and Bathsheba. As Hardy's later fiction demonstrates even more tragically, the countryside could no longer be used to buffer England against the risks and uncertainties of its commercial dealings.

Gender, sexuality, and the writer

The pastoral was becoming equated with the past, and perhaps with a peculiarly feminine sensibility which seemed increasingly at odds with the needs of the age. George Eliot died in December 1880, and in her obituaries she is celebrated principally as a chronicler of the Warwickshire countryside in which she had grown up. This tendency is explicitly gendered by Leslie Stephen, who writes of the delight of the freshness of her first works, such as *Scenes of Clerical Life*, *Adam Bede* and *Silas Marner* (1861), and of the 'singular charm [springing] out of the tender affection which reproduces the little world left so far behind and hallowed by the romance of early association'.[15] While describing Eliot as 'the greatest woman who ever won literary fame' and 'one of the very few writers of our day to whom the name "great" could be conceded with any plausibility' (p. 152), he describes her demise as marking 'the termination of the great period of English fiction which began with Scott' (p. 152), and thus intimately associates her fame and talent with looking backward to a period in which such feminine talents could have their place. The gendering of Stephen's appreciation is consistent with the analogy between literary and social discourses (which he elaborated in an article on 'The Moral Element in Literature' 1881 – see extract 3, p. 138), and in which he wrote: 'To study literature is not merely (as has been said) to know what has been best said by the greatest men, but to learn to know those men themselves.'[16] Six years later, in 1887, he developed the analogy further when he wrote that reading should be thought of in terms of making 'the personal acquaintance of men better, wiser, more highly endowed than ourselves'; it is a relationship to be conducted at the convenience of readers who 'can put [the author] in our pockets, admit him to an audience when we are in the humour, and treat him as familiarly as a college chum'.[17] It is unlikely that a woman writer, even a George Eliot, would be admitted to such a relationship.

Stephen's writings are part of a tendency at the time to render the writing of fiction more masculine, something also effected by the establishment of the Society of Authors in 1884, a professional body largely modelled on existing, male London clubs. Following the 1880 Education Act, which built on Forster in making elementary education compulsory in England and Wales, there was a growing realization that fiction would take up a significant part of new readers' time; indeed a survey of the Manchester Public Library in 1886 revealed that the 12 most frequently borrowed books were all novels. *The Origin of Species* was also well liked: it circulated 'almost like a popular novel'.[18] In such a context, and particularly in the light of the increased availability of fiction within the proliferating public libraries, the novelist became a figure of increased social responsibility. As Robert Louis Stevenson writes, 'the sum of the contemporary knowledge or ignorance of good and evil is, in large measure, the handiwork of those who write'.[19]

A number of factors combined to suggest that the exemplary novelist should be a masculine one. Commentators feared that the huge number of women novelists of the time were pushing men out of the market, but, more importantly, women were in the vanguard of the proponents of a new range of social configurations. As middle-class women's employment opportunities increased in the wake of their admission to higher education, so the appeal of marriage, with its attendant legal and financial limitations, declined. It is perhaps because of this that the second Married Women's Property Act was passed in 1882. Following a long-standing campaign by a variously constituted married women's property committee, which had been working since 1855, the 1882 Act finally made equal the property rights and responsibilities of all women regardless of marital status. But marriage was also being challenged as a result of the proliferation of birth control material in the late 1870s and early 1880s. In 1877 and 1878 Annie Besant and Charles Bradlaugh were prosecuted for publishing birth-control material which was sufficiently cheap as to be available to most sections of the population. The trials themselves, of course, gave welcome publicity to the birth-control movement. The fears associated with birth control were two-fold: first, that a decline in the birth rate (which did take place in the early 1880s) would weaken both Britain's industrial strength and the country's defences should it need to engage in war; and, second, the effect of contra-ception on newly educated women might, especially in the light of George Eliot's example, encourage them not to marry at all, but rather to live fulfilled single, professional, but not celibate lives. More profoundly, of course, the possibility that women might shun child-bearing attacked the very basis of sexual difference on which Victorian social institutions were founded.

It is interesting to note that the figure of the actress becomes more respectable at this time. Henry Irving had taken over the Lyceum theatre in 1878, and, with his architecturally sumptuous productions and acclaimed productions of Shakespeare, had done much to heighten the theatre's social and artistic standing. But his theatre's greatest attraction was his leading lady Ellen Terry, almost universally acclaimed as charming, no matter what her part: only her Lady Macbeth in 1888 defied the critics' adulation. Such a charming actress actually advertised an appropriately attractive form of femininity, which was economically guaranteed by her audiences' presence. The actress was crucially, as Eliza Lynn Linton puts it, 'not unfeminine', and her occupation less likely 'to damage the inherent modesties of woman's nature [than] the discussions of doubtful subjects before a mixed audience, which more than one of our lady-lecturers [Josephine Butler perhaps] has done'.[20] Such considerations seemed to outweigh the ambiguities of the actress's independent, professional status. The visual arts respond even more conservatively to contemporary concerns, with a proliferation of images of confined women, such as John William Waterhouse's 'Saint Eulalia' (1885), Herbert Schmalz's 'Faithful Unto Death' (1888), and Frederic Leighton's 'Captive Andromache' (1886–88). Leighton, at that time President of the Royal Academy (which he led from 1878 until his death in 1898), further confined his women within classically derived draperies and narratives, and within a technique which effectively smoothed out any traces of a textured skin, substituting instead the finish of a marble statue.

Critics were concerned too that the form of male identity being promoted by fiction should be of an appropriate kind, for this was also the period when the threat of effeminacy, most prominently associated at the time with Oscar Wilde, began to emerge. A *Punch* cartoon of 1881 shows a languorous 'Maudle', clearly modelled on Wilde, talking to a Mrs Brown about the profession her son might follow:

Maudle. 'HOW CONSUMMATELY LOVELY YOUR SON IS, MRS BROWN!'
Mrs Brown (a Philistine from the country). 'WHAT? HE'S A NICE, MANLY BOY, IF YOU MEAN THAT, MR MAUDLE. HE HAS JUST LEFT SCHOOL, YOU KNOW, AND WISHES TO BE AN ARTIST.'
Maudle. 'WHY SHOULD HE BE AN ARTIST?'
Mrs Brown. 'WELL, HE MUST BE SOMETHING!'
Maudle. 'WHY SHOULD HE BE ANYTHING? WHY NOT LET HIM REMAIN FOR EVER CONTENT TO EXIST BEAUTIFULLY!'
(Mrs Brown determines that at all events her Son shall not study Art under Maudle.)[21]

Though the term 'homosexuality' did not achieve currency in English until 1892,[22] 'inversion' was a phenomenon generating increasing anxiety. Sexually, then, there was a proliferation of discourses concerned to articulate a new recognition of the multiple possibilities of how sexuality was experienced.

In terms of fiction, the debate about the person of the author dominated two novels from 1885, George Meredith's *Diana of the Crossways* and Eliza Lynn Linton's *The Autobiography of Christopher Kirkland*, a novel narrated by the eponymous first-person hero, but which was recognizably based on the life of Lynn Linton herself, and which unsettled reviewers with its gender-transpositions. Meredith's Diana was based on the novelist and poet Caroline Norton, who, following a messy separation from her husband, and his very public and unproven allegations in 1836 of her adultery with the then Prime Minister Lord Melbourne, became a highly successful campaigner for women's rights to their children, and for divorce. Within Meredith's novel, Diana uses her fiction to explore the dilemmas of her position as a woman forced to be economically independent, and whose isolation renders her vulnerable to sexual suspicion. It also, perhaps in spite of Meredith's intentions, raises the issue of how far women were allowed to be artistically autonomous. He rather employs Diana's fiction as a form of confessional diary, a mirror of her moods, than as a medium for her own creativity. Lynn Linton's tortured novel was more unsettling, in that its adoption of a male voice for a woman's story explicitly respects the gender-conventions of her society, but obviously shows up those conventions as meaningless. The male persona both absorbs and confirms Lynn Linton's aberrant position.

Politically, too, the early 1880s were years of reorientation and realignment which generated some considerable anxieties, for in this, as indeed in the sexual arena, there were signs not only of change, but of attempts to overthrow existing structures and hierarchies. The year 1884, for instance, saw the formation of both the Social Democratic Federation (SDF, formerly the Democratic Federation) and the Fabian Society. The numbers involved in these groups were not great – estimates suggest that there were at most 3,000 members of socialist organizations in the mid-1880s (Hoppen, *Mid-Victorian Generation*, p. 650) – but they were nonetheless feared by the establishment, particularly within the prevailing context of unrest. The SDF was felt unlikely to make much progress in parliament, though it did contest two seats in the general election of 1885, gaining a total of 59 votes, and achieved most notoriety later in the decade when it capitalized upon workers' unrest in meetings in London in 1886 and 1887 (see Chapter 4 below). Like many early socialist groups, however, the SDF was riven by internal disagreements, and lost many of its most prominent members, including Eleanor Marx and William Morris in 1885, the last of whom went on to found the Socialist League. By contrast, the Fabians were not concerned directly with parliament, but rather with debating the practical measures needed to bring about a more just society, and with gathering the social information needed to facilitate reform. They believed rather in 'gradualism through propaganda and through the election of Fabians to various bodies of local government'.[23] Small wonder then that H.M. Hyndman, the founder of the SDF, called them 'The Micawber club' (Wood, *Nineteenth-Century Britain*, p. 366). But the socialist movement was significant in opening up the political scene to include another tranche of opinion, in bringing the views of Marx (who had died in 1883) into clearer public focus, and in laying the foundations for the formation of the Independent Labour Party in 1893.

In Ireland, too, the stability of English rule was being contested in the wake of the development of the Home Rule movement, which formally began with the formation of the Home Rule League in 1873. At this period, Ireland was effectively governed as another colony, with a viceroy-equivalent in its Lord Lieutenant, and with an imported administration based in Dublin Castle which was backed up by a 12,000-strong paramilitary police force and 25,000 troops. As was the case in India, Anglicization was a central tenet of Britain's education policy in Ireland.[24] Set up in response to this situation, and in the wake of disappointment with the Land Act of 1870, the Home Rule movement soon gathered further support as bad harvests, falling prices, and the threat of potato failures in 1878 and 1879 revived memories of the Great Famine, and generated hardships for farmers, evictions of whom rose from 463 in 1877 to 2110 in 1880.[25] The violence of the so-called 'Land War' reached its height between 1879 and 1882, the latter year seeing the murder in Dublin's Phoenix Park of the government's chief secretary and under-secretary. A Land Act had been introduced in 1881, but was not sufficient fully to quell the country's agitation. In 1885, Gladstone, who had personally intervened in the Irish question, made a startling conversion to Home Rule for the Irish, and thus precipitated what many saw as a sea-change in the relationship between Britain and her colonies. The mere envisaging of Home Rule suggested the possibility of the disintegration of an Empire whose coherence was based on a sense of possession. By 1886, Hoppen suggests, 'Irish considerations had begun to reshape the character of British politics' (*Mid-Victorian Generation*, p. 590).

Out of Africa

Before this time, however, the colonies promised to provide, if not a solution to, then at least a respite from the challenges of domestic politics. The 'Scramble for Africa', though predicated upon a competition between the European nations for strategic control of the African continent, gave Britain an outlet for political and economic expansionism and a space in which it could work vigorously to defend its interests. As we will see, Africa also provided the arena for the most significant novels to come out of the early 1880s.

The partition of Africa was directly related to the state of Europe at the time. As countries such as Germany and Italy became unified, so they were able to garner the strength to challenge Britain's international supremacy, and to move into Africa as a valuable market for Europe's rapidly expanding exports trade. Clearly, Britain had to protect its trading interests, but had also to ensure that it was not left behind in the new phase of African annexation. Trade routes as well as markets had to be secured, lest rivals took advantage. Furthermore, as European rivals competed more fiercely for continental markets, so the African outlets became commensurably more significant, especially in the light of the competition increasingly being felt from Russia and the USA, whose sheer size and resources meant that only by expanding its effective borders into the continent of Africa could Britain hope to keep up with them.

Africa was also a significant source of raw materials for British consumption, providing 85 per cent of the world's ivory, and one third of its rubber,[26] and the supply of such goods needed to be protected from both the activities of freelance adventurers and the instabilities of the uncertain control of power in the continent in the late nineteenth century. Local disputes and an expansionist and militant Islamic movement were prompting European powers to move in to fill what they perceived as a power vacuum. Britain was also concerned that African disputes should not expand to draw European powers into conflict with each other, hence again the need for interventionist policies. And, finally, the precariousness of the domestic situation in Britain gave an additional urgency to its activities abroad. There was a common belief that without the markets of the Empire British trade would collapse, precipitating thousands into poverty and unemployment. Interestingly, the colonies are also invoked at this time, as they were earlier in the century, as a place to which the excess British population might go, though now that excess is one determined rather by poverty than immorality.[27] Britain's settlements might also, in the words of James Froude, provide an antidote to the enervations of city living, and:

> where there was still soil and sunshine boundless and life-giving [the country might] renew its mighty youth, bring forth as many millions as it would, and would still have the means to breed and rear them strong as the best which she had produced in her early prime.[28]

For all these reasons, then, Africa took on extraordinary significance for Britain in a period of depression at home, and of anxieties about its masculinity, and its international status.

Britain was also active in Egypt and the Sudan at this time, but it is in central and southern Africa that fiction found both a newly compelling set of situations and an answer to the anxieties about appropriate authorship that were being debated. A new breed of adventure stories emerged which capitalized on the opportunities emanating out of Africa to create a newly virile form of popular fiction. In 1887, H. Rider Haggard wrote that English fiction was currently 'at the mercy of the Young Person, and a dreadful nuisance most of us find her'. He wonders:

> Why do *men* hardly ever read a novel? Because, in ninety-nine cases out of a hundred, it is utterly false as a picture of life. . . . The ordinary popular English novel represents life as it is considered desirable that schoolgirls should suppose it to be. Consequently it is for the most part rubbish, without a spark of vitality about it, for no novel written on those false lines will live.[29]

Such considerations, along with the international situation, provide the context for Rider Haggard's *King Solomon's Mines* (1885), a bloodthirsty romance and quest narrative, in which, true to its genre, women scarcely appear, except in the form of Foulata the beautiful, but soon to be dead, native girl, and Gagool, an ancient and malevolent occult figure, who also dies shortly after fatally wounding Foulata.

The narrative concerns the dual search for the diamonds of the eponymous mines, and for the brother of the English aristocrat (Sir Henry Curtis) who funds the expedition; and is narrated in the first person by Allan Quatermain, an elephant-hunter and seasoned veteran of African adventures. It is a fiction written expressly for 'big and little boys' as its dedication declares, but which has some profoundly adult anxieties. Along with Captain Good, and their indigenous servants, the men make a perilous journey across deserts and mountains before reaching the land of the Kukuana, where the diamonds are alleged to be, and for which place Sir Henry's brother was also heading. Along the way, the travellers go elephant-hunting, something which was both economic necessity and sport at the time:

> Now was our opportunity, and firing away as quickly as we could load, we killed five of the poor beasts, and no doubt should have bagged the whole herd, had they not suddenly given up their attempts to climb the bank and rushed headlong down the nullah. We were too tired to follow them, and perhaps also a little sick of slaughter, eight elephants being a pretty good bag for one day.
>
> So after we were rested a little, and the Kafirs had cut out the hearts of two of the dead elephants for supper, we started homewards, very well pleased with ourselves, having made up our minds to send the bearers on the morrow to chop out the tusks.[30]

The distressing hunting scenes are just a prelude, however, to what will follow. Arriving in Kukuana, the men's attentions are diverted to the necessity of replacing the barbarous king with the rightful heir, their own servant Umbopa, and of installing just rule in the country, which is achieved through the novel's set piece, an extraordinarily bloody battle, in which many thousands of men are killed, and in which the virile Sir Henry plays a major part, culminating in his decapitating the corrupt King Twala.

As far as it goes, this part of the narrative might seem to confirm European supremacy and justice through the recourse to a frequently invoked Christianity and sense of justice which is literally embodied in the splendid frame of Sir Henry. However, it is also a narrative in which the British men have to confront several contemporary anxieties which take shape, often literally, within Africa. The very geography of the place needs to be subdued, and it is not accidental that much of that geography is specifically gendered female. The first range of mountains that the men have to cross are shaped like 'Sheba's breasts', and seem the most conspicuously brooding female presence in the text. The men's underground search for the cave of treasure, their near-immurement in the mountain, and escape down various labyrinthine tunnels is akin to a nightmarish birth-experience. Furthermore, for all the fun that is made of the credulity of the natives, who are encouraged to believe that the white men come from the sky and are to be worshipped as gods, these indigenous peoples represent for the British a form of atavism, which is also invoked in references to Sir Henry being like a marvellous Dane (p. 5, ch. 1), and which bring them all too close to the fears of degeneration beginning to emerge in Britain, and which have to be bested in Africa. As Patrick Brantlinger argues, '[t]he atavistic descents into the primitive experienced by fictional characters seem often to be allegories of the larger regressive movement of civilization, British progress transformed into British backsliding'.[31] Haggard's heroes have in Twala not only an enemy who represents the worst excesses of a corrupt, decaying, and superstitious civilization, but also the opportunity to subdue that enemy by a display of physical courage not often seen, and not often needed, within Britain's own increasingly enervated society. Ironically, perhaps, this is represented as a form of visceral recidivism, but one which can then be transformed at home into the more conventional signifier of a pair of elephant tusks.

Not dissimilar fantasies are played out in Robert Louis Stevenson's *Treasure Island* (1883), where, in a search for the treasure buried by Captain Flint, the mutinying crew themselves take on the role of the primitive savages who have to be outwitted by superior intelligence and planning, thus making more explicit that the journey into Africa or the tropical island is essentially a journey into a feared and repressed capacity within the British themselves. Again written for boys of all ages, the short novel was originally intended as a present for Stevenson's 12-year-old stepson Lloyd Osbourne, and apart from the fleeting figure of the mother of Jim Hawkins, the novel's young hero, this is another all-male text where women are entirely absent as markers of male identity. All the relationships are defined by and within male centres, most notably that of the ship, the Hispaniola. Away from English shores, the men are freed from the need to model their social arrangements on the domestic space, and consequently adopt new social forms which privilege the adventurous and daring. Both novels reward their British adventurers by enabling them to return home with great wealth which in some way insulates them from the pressures of a domestic setting, and indeed, in the case of Rider Haggard's men, enables them to re-establish their all-male menage at home. These are novels which are both in retreat from fears of decline at home, and which see the solution to those fears in a mixture of the assertion of masculinity and the forceful repression of aberrance. Ironically, of course, Stevenson's greatest success would come with his novella *The Strange Case of Dr Jekyll and Mr Hyde* (1886), which investigates precisely the return of the repressed, atavistic sexual and feminized instincts of Dr Jekyll in the persona of Mr Hyde.

However, perhaps the most interesting novel to come, literally, out of Africa at this period was also one of the most extraordinary of the whole century. Olive Schreiner's *The Story of an African Farm* (1883) was written while Schreiner was working as a governess in the Cape Colony in 1876. She came to England in 1881, bringing her manuscript with her. After initial disappointments, the novel was published by Chapman and Hall, at the recommendation of their reader, George Meredith. Schreiner's novel takes the figure of the female orphan, Lyndall, and shows her garnering an education from the resources available to her on the farm run by her dead father's wife, Tant Sannie. She grows up with her cousin, Em, and the son of the farm's German overseer, Waldo, as together they negotiate the difficulties of love and sexual attraction in a context which teaches them only of selfishness and of the easiest forms of gratification. Lyndall seeks intellectual stimulation and satisfaction through the study of her father's old books, and through the boarding school she later attends, but finds there only an education which 'finish[ed] everything but imbecility and weakness'.[32] While there she tries to write, and 'finds out how hard it is to make your thoughts look like anything but imbecile fools when you paint them with ink on paper' (p. 185), and in any case an audience for ideas would be lacking. Even Waldo, her closest companion, cannot really hear her: 'To him [her] words were no confession, no glimpse into the strong, proud, restless heart of the woman. They were general words with a general application' (p. 217, pt. 2, ch. 6).

Against this background of disappointed intellectual ambitions, Lyndall meets and falls pregnant by a stranger whom, though he is eventually willing to marry Lyndall, she rejects in favour of trying to bear and bring up the baby by herself, thus adding a contemporary focus to the figure of the seduced young woman. In a harrowing scene, Lyndall gives birth to a still-born baby, and dies herself shortly afterwards. Her story is a starkly told tale of aspirations disappointed both in terms of love and intellectual ambition, and revives much of the despair of Maggie Tulliver's fate, of a young woman born into a place which can barely recognize, let alone satisfy, her longings. The fundamental difference between Eliot and Schreiner, however, and indeed between their respective generations, is that Schreiner was going further in questioning the basis and viability of sexual attraction as currently experienced and understood. She represents it as necessarily dangerous and distracting, and tries in her writings at the time to evolve a new understanding and possible structure for male–female relations. In *African Farm*, she gives us the character of Gregory Rose, ostensibly a suitor for Em's hand, who falls in love with Lyndall and, realizing she will never love him sexually, decides instead to devote himself to caring for her when she leaves the farm to have her baby. In order to nurse her, Rose has to abandon his masculine identity, and to masquerade as a female nurse, which he successfully does. As Ruth First and Anne Scott suggest, Gregory Rose is 'the novel's attempt at some kind of androgynous resolution to the problem of sexual differentiation'.[33]

Out of this African novel, then, comes not an assertion of an exaggerated form of masculinity but the suggestion that at the heart of every person is a fundamental androgyny which might provide the resolution to the novel's examination of the problem of trying to reconcile mental and physical aspirations, intellectual and romantic attraction. The androgyne had for some time been a figure of social anxiety – it was in part the 'Girl of the Period's' penchant for male slang which Eliza Lynn Linton had deplored – and would become so to an even greater extent again in the 1890s, with the social spectres of the dandy and the New Woman. The blurring of sexual identities seemed increasingly to impinge on a range of different spheres, professional and cultural, as well as sexual. While represented in *The Story of an African Farm* as concerning primarily personal and emotional aspirations, it figured outside fiction as part of a growing anxiety with the health of the nation and, to borrow Karl Pearson's phrase, with the 'race-instinct for reproduction'.[34]

Pearson was a friend of Schreiner, a mathematician and an early eugenicist who was the figure behind the establishment of the 'Men and Women's Club', which was founded in 1885 to 'talk about sex'.[35] In the first paper presented to the 20-strong club (10 men and 10 women, who included Olive Schreiner), Pearson wrote with some anxiety of the new sexual and social freedoms being enjoyed particularly by educated women, and suggested that, in denying their child-bearing role, they were fundamentally denying their sexual identity. He feared that if such women chose either to have children outside marriage or not to have children at all, society would suffer, whether in its laws (of inheritance) and its structures, or in its 'race-predominance' ('The Woman's Question', p. 389). Like other contemporary commentators, Pearson saw both the source of and solution to Britain's current perceived decline in sexual practices, and specifically in women's attentiveness to their child-bearing responsibilities. It was all very well to be a childless, unmarried, but sexually active George Eliot (who was in the public eye again with the 1885 publication of her husband J.W. Cross's memoir of the novelist), but her example actually entailed the most potentially devastating critique of the economic organization of society.

Pearson concluded that, even if the price for race-predominance were the further subjection of women, it should be paid in order that Britain might retain its position in the world with a healthy and growing populace. He ends his paper by suggesting that centuries of women's subjection might actually have been a blessing in preparing them to put aside their own ambitions and unselfishly to 'submit [their] liberty to the restraints demanded by social welfare, and to the conditions imposed by race-permanence' ('The Woman's Question', p. 394). Unsurprisingly the paper was highly controversial, and was criticized by Schreiner for concentrating solely on women, while discussing 'man only as far as he throws light upon her question. This is entirely wrong' (quoted in Walkowitz, *City of Dreadful Delight*, p. 149). It is most significant, however, in demonstrating two things: first, the extent to which explicit discussion of sexual matters was now possible, thanks in large part to the work of Josephine Butler and her campaigns against the Contagious Diseases Acts (which had been suspended in 1883, prior to being repealed in 1886); and, second, the strength of the contemporary interest in policing the appropriate expression of sexual desire and activity.

In the same year, the journalist W.T. Stead had published his notorious series of articles on 'The Maiden Tribute of Modern Babylon' in the *Pall Mall Gazette*, in which he revealed how easy it was to buy child-prostitutes in the streets of modern London. The articles caused an outrage, in part because Stead was imprisoned for his part in the procuring of a girl to prove the point of his articles, but principally because they highlighted the proximity of vice and virtue on the London streets, and brought that proximity to bear in the homes of readers. It foregrounded, too, the extent of the trade of prostitution in London. The legislative effect of Stead's work was felt in the Criminal Law Amendment Act, the so-called Labouchère Amendment, which was passed in 1885 and which raised the age of sexual consent from 13 to 16, and made procuration a criminal offence. It also introduced new penalties for private as well as public homosexual activities, and in 1895 became the means by which Oscar Wilde was prosecuted. All these events contributed to make of 1885 what Jeffrey Weeks has described as an 'annus mirabilis of sexual politics',[36] a year in which a wealth of sexual discourses and discussions was unleashed to be greeted by a legislative attempt to combat non-productive, socially unhealthy sexual practices. These events occurred against a background of economic depression, and increasing political unrest, which saw the passing of the third Reform Act (which enfranchised farm labourers) in 1884, continuing unrest in Ireland, and, perhaps most devastatingly, the death of a national hero, General Gordon, in Khartoum in January 1885. He had gone there to evacuate

British forces, but, against orders, had stayed to try to enforce discipline in the unruly country. His death seemed to herald the end for the Empire.

Thus, in 1885, anxieties about Empire, economics, sexuality and the family coalesce, and find their fictional counterparts in *King Solomon's Mines*, in Meredith's *Diana of the Crossways* (published in book form in 1885), and in Lynn Linton's *The Autobiography of Christopher Kirkland*. Also in that year, in George Moore's account of a drunken wife and disastrously tawdry marriage in *A Mummer's Wife*, the country saw the beginning of the influence on British writers of the naturalistic novels of Zola, whose *Nana* had been translated and published in England by Henry Vizetelly in 1884. In these novels by Meredith, Lynn Linton, and Moore, some of the concerns of the *fin de siècle* were already being sounded. And in George Moore's observance of the influence of Zola, and of Flaubert before him, French naturalism merged with English realism to produce novels which dealt viscerally with the darker side of life, with drunkenness, with violence, with the indignities of work, and with the minutely told details of squalid urban poverty. In literary, economic, and political terms, 1885 was almost unrecognizably far removed from the confident heyday of Britain's industrial prosperity.

Notes

1 The first football international was held between England and Scotland in Scotland, and the score was 0–0. England and Australia played the first test match in England at the Oval. England's team on that occasion included W.G. Grace.
2 Quoted in A. Sanders, *Dickens and the Spirit of the Age* (Oxford, 1999), p. 63.
3 George Eliot, *Middlemarch* (Harmondsworth, 1994), p. 560, ch. 56.
4 Review of *Middlemarch* in the *Fortnightly Review*, January 1873, quoted in David Carroll, *George Eliot: The Critical Heritage* (London, 1971), pp. 331–8 (p. 332).
5 Letter of 10? December 1871, in Gordon S. Haight, ed., *The George Eliot Letters*, Vol. 9 (9 vols, New Haven and London, 1954–78), p. 33.
6 Gillian Beer, *George Eliot* (Brighton, 1986), p. 201.
7 Henry James, review of *Middlemarch*, *Galaxy*, quoted in *Critical Heritage*, pp. 353–9 (p. 359).
8 K. Theodore Hoppen, *The Mid-Victorian Generation, 1846–1886* (Oxford, 1998), p. 305.
9 *Ibid.*, p. 306.
10 R.C.K. Ensor, *England, 1870–1914* (Oxford, 1936), p. 115.
11 See John Sutherland, 'Introduction' to Anthony Trollope, *The Way We Live Now* (Oxford, 1982), pp. vii–xxviii (p. xix).
12 George Eliot, *Daniel Deronda* (Harmondsworth, 1995), p. 49, ch. 5.
13 Hugh Witemeyer, *George Eliot and the Visual Arts* (New Haven and London, 1979), p. 99.
14 Thomas Hardy, *Far From the Madding Crowd* (Harmondsworth, 1978), p. 195, ch. 22.

15 Leslie Stephen, 'George Eliot', *Cornhill Magazine*, 43 (1881), 152–68 (pp. 155, 156).

16 Leslie Stephen, 'The Moral Element in English Literature', *Cornhill Magazine*, 43 (1881), 34–50 (p. 50).

17 Leslie Stephen, 'The Study of English Literature', *Cornhill Magazine*, n.s. 8 (1887), 486–508 (p. 486). As Chris Baldick points out, the education pioneer F.D. Maurice also based his theory of literature's value on its ability to provide the reader with personal friends (*The Social Mission of English Criticism, 1848–1932* (Oxford, 1983), pp. 74–5).

18 E.C. Whitehurst, 'What and How to Read', *Westminster Review*, n.s. 70 (1886), 99–118 (p. 117). The 12 most frequently borrowed books were *Pickwick Papers* 389 times, *Bleak House* 361, *David Copperfield* 303, *Robinson Crusoe* 294, *Oliver Twist* 278, *Martin Chuzzlewit* 224, *The Mill on the Floss* 217, *The Arabian Nights* 211, *Ivanhoe* 200, *Vanity Fair* 195, *East Lynne* 188, *Adam Bede* 181.

19 Robert Louis Stevenson, 'The Morality of the Profession of Letters', *Fortnightly Review*, n.s. 29 (1881), 513–20 (p. 515).

20 E. Lynn Linton, 'The Stage as a Profession for Women', *National Review*, 5 (1885), 8–19 (pp. 14, 12).

21 'Maudle on the Choice of a Profession', *Punch,* 80 (1881).

22 The term was coined by C.G. Chaddock in his translation of Richard von Krafft-Ebing's *Psychopathia Sexualis* (1889), a pioneering series of sexual case-studies.

23 A. Wood, *Nineteenth-Century Britain, 1815–1914* (Harlow, 2nd edn, 1982), p. 366.

24 Andrew Porter, 'The Empire and the World', in C. Matthew, ed., *The Nineteenth Century, 1815–1901* (Oxford, 2000), pp. 135–62 (p. 145).

25 Howard Martin, *Britain in the Nineteenth Century* (Walton-on-Thames, 1996), p. 349.

26 R. Hyam, *Britain's Imperial Century, 1815–1914* (Basingstoke, 2nd edn, 1993), p. 218.

27 For more details, see Bernard Porter, *The Lion's Share: A Short History of British Imperialism, 1850–1995* (London, 1996), pp. 79–80. Details of the Scramble for Africa given in this paragraph are drawn largely from Porter, pp. 74–84, and Hyam, *Britain's Imperial Century*, pp. 213–31.

28 J.A. Froude, *Oceana* (1886); quoted in Bernard Porter, *The Lion's Share*, p. 80.

29 H. Rider Haggard, 'About Fiction', *Contemporary Review*, 51 (1887), 172–80 (p. 177).

30 H. Rider Haggard, *King Solomon's Mines* (Harmondsworth, 1994), p. 53, ch. 4.

31 P. Brantlinger, *Rule of Darkness: British Literature and Imperialism, 1830–1914* (Ithaca and London), p. 229.

32 Olive Schreiner, *The Story of an African Farm* (Harmondsworth, 1971), p. 185, pt. 2, ch. 4.

33 Ruth First and Anne Scott, *Olive Schreiner* (London, 1980), p. 106.

34 Karl Pearson, 'The Woman's Question' (1885), in *The Ethic of Freethought: A Selection of Essays and Lectures* (London, 1888), pp. 370–94 (p. 389).

35 Judith R. Walkowitz, *City of Dreadful Delight: Narratives of Sexual Danger in Late-Victorian London* (Chicago, 1992), p. 135.

36 Jeffrey Weeks, *Sex, Politics and Society: The Regulation of Sexuality since 1800* (London and New York, 1981), p. 87.

|4|

1886–1901
'Fin de siècle? Fin du globe'

The end of the century proved to be an anxious time, one marked by fears of decline and change, which were often represented as a fear of the new. The age of the 'new', the new journalism, new drama, new woman, did little to excite the self-proclaimed Philistines who saw in such developments a descent from classical ideals and a catering to popular tastes which could only mean the degradation of British culture. Underlying all perhaps was the fear surrounding the fact that the century was drawing to a close. An ending confers meaning, gives the final chapter which can provide the key to the significance of all that has preceded it, can reveal the foregoing narrative as one of worthy integrity, or as an ironically purblind journey into disillusionment and disappointed expectations. Thus, not only the status and legacy of their own times but of that of the whole century often seemed to be at stake in the opposition between Philistines and dandies, new and 'old' women, socialists and conservatives, which marked the last 15 combative and highly contested years of the Victorian period. The whole notion of legacy was further complicated by the plays of Ibsen, and in particular *Ghosts* (written in 1881, and performed in London in 1891) which saw an innocent child inheriting the syphilitic symptoms of its dissolute father. For those, like the new woman, who saw freedom available only in a cutting loose from legacies of the past, Ibsen's analysis was heady and exhilarating; for others, his assessment threatened to send society into a moral freefall.

Freed from the authoritativeness foisted upon, or often claimed by, the realist novelists of the earlier part of the century, the novelists of the *fin de siècle* experimented with naturalist fictions, and with narratives which invoked fantasy or myth in treating of the concerns of their period. In their turn Bram Stoker's Dracula, Stevenson's Jekyll and Hyde, and George du Maurier's Svengali have become figures of modern mythology, drawing upon the developments of modern psychology in figuring what Freud would come to term the return of the repressed. Though little known in Britain until the early twentieth century, we can see how Freud's theories of dreams and of the unconscious develop in parallel with what British novelists were articulating. The fears which they invoke may also, however, be seen within the more available contexts of Britain's social and economic position in the 1890s, a position which gave much cause for concern, and which found an answering anxiety within the home as domestic structures, too, felt the force of change. The novel mapped out, but also fed, these changes as it experimented with new shapes and forms, and as it found itself challenged by the new popularity of the short story.

The streets of London

At the end of *Middlemarch*, on hearing that Dorothea is to move to London, Celia plaintively cries out, 'How can you always live in a street?' (p. 821, ch. 84). By 1886, the objection would have seemed as eccentric as it does to us now. The urban experience was well established as the norm, and the street was the space in which people expected to live, work, and display their identities, to mingle with other classes, and to conduct their transactions. In the late 1880s, however, the streets of London developed new narratives of sexual danger and political anarchy which were to define their presence in narratives of the late nineteenth century. The city was home to political societies and discussion groups, such as the socialists and Fabians, who sought to unpick by various means existing conditions, conditions which themselves became the focus of investigations resulting in the publication of Charles Booth's *Life and Labour of the People in London* (1889–1903), which revealed that around a third of Londoners lived in poverty. No longer confined to the East End, they were spread throughout the city.

The recognition of this mingling of classes is part of a reconfiguration of the city which took place at this period, and was itself part of a greater revolution in the understanding of human psychology and class relations. In *The Princess Casamassima* (1886), Henry James writes of the possibilities of revolutionary insurrection in late-Victorian Britain thus:

> Nothing of it appears above the surface; but there's an immense underworld peopled with a thousand forms of revolutionary passion and devotion. ... And on top of it all society lives. People come and go, and buy and sell, and drink and dance, and make money and make love, and seem to know nothing and suspect nothing and think of

nothing. . . . All that's one half of it; the other half is that every thing's doomed! In silence, in darkness, but under the feet of every one of us, the revolution lives and works.[1]

James's figuring of a netherworld anticipates the horrors of H.G. Wells's *The Time Machine* (1895), a time-travel fantasy inspired by Wells's dismay at contemporary conditions, in which a class of brutalized and etiolated Morlocks live underground and feed off the inbred and degenerating Eloi. But James also signals the apprehension of a closer and more unstable relation between social groups than has previously figured in Victorian fiction, an apprehension which actively takes on the forms of the newly made city, with its developing underground system and its highly permeable geographical boundaries.

The fear of revolution was fuelled in 1886 and 1887 by a series of inflammatory political meetings in Trafalgar Square, named of course for previous national glories. On 8 February 1886, the SDF held a meeting in the Square, which was being used at the same time by the Labourers' League, who were addressing the cause of the skilled unemployed, and by the Free Trade League. Fighting broke out between the different groups, and, as the police failed to maintain order among a crowd estimated to be 15–20,000 strong, SDF marchers escaped their control and rioted in Pall Mall and Mayfair, breaking windows, and bringing socialism to the heart of London's clubland and aristocratic centre. Queen Victoria allegedly described the 'monstrous riot' as 'a momentary triumph for socialism and a disgrace to the capital' (quoted in Beckson, *London in the 1890s*, p. 14). It is worth noting, however, that, far from being the preserve of the needy, socialism was being widely debated in literary society, and provided the inspiration for William Morris's 1890 novel *News from Nowhere*, and for Oscar Wilde's essay 'The Soul of Man Under Socialism' (1891), where he reiterates Ruskin's assertion in *Unto This Last* that the only real wealth is the life that one lives: 'Your perfection is inside of you. If you could realise that, you would not want to be rich. Ordinary riches can be stolen from you. Real riches cannot.'[2]

In 1887, also of course the year of Victoria's Golden Jubilee, socialist interests coincided with the ever troubling Irish question, and on 13 November, or, as it came to be known, Bloody Sunday, protesters tried to converge on Trafalgar Square to protest at the arrest of the Irish MP William O'Brien, and to campaign for the right to free speech. Few marchers were allowed to reach the Square for the rally, however, as they were charged by police before they got there. Two out of the 100 injured demonstrators died, and two organizers (including a Scottish MP) were sentenced to six weeks in jail. Later in the decade, working-class feelings were more effectively marshalled by the trade union movement in major strikes, such as that of the match girls in 1888 and the London dock strike of 1889.

By that time, the London streets were also subject to another kind of fear: in the autumn of 1888 Jack the Ripper struck, killing five women in the Whitechapel area. The unsolved murders, of a particularly brutal and disturbing kind, involving the partial dissection of the victims' internal and external genital organs, attracted attention throughout the capital, and once again insisted on the consanguinity of London's different areas. This affinity is underlined in the controversies and speculations over the identity of the Ripper, which included 'a Russian Jewish anarchist, a policeman, a local denizen of Whitechapel, an erotic maniac of the "upper classes" of society, a religious fanatic, a mad doctor, [and] a scientific sociologist'.[3] Though Whitechapel was notorious as a place of overcrowding and poverty, where foreign immigrants, and particularly Jews, lived alongside hostile neighbours, and starvation wages forced many women into prostitution, it was also the case that by 1888, as *The Times* reported, 'the Whitechapel murderers and their victims are neighbours of every Londoner' (quoted in Walkowitz, *City of Dreadful Delight*, p. 195). Whether made so by intensive reporting of the case or by upper-class slumming incursions into the area, Whitechapel was no longer represented as absolutely foreign, as was, for instance, Tom All-Alone's in *Bleak House*. In *The Picture of Dorian Gray* (1891), Wilde has his aristocratic hero frequent the East End for his descents into the pleasures which leave his portrait looking so bloated with vice.

The terror of the city is best represented in a story which pre-dates the Trafalgar Square and Ripper disturbances, but which tellingly extends their connotations of a complication of urban identity into the individual psyche, thus drawing on recent developments in psychology, and giving the period one of its most influential and telling figurations of a divided self in the characters or character of Dr Jekyll and Mr Hyde. Robert Louis Stevenson's novella was published in January 1886, and revealed a London of highly permeable spaces, of networks of unexpected relationships, where respectability and absolute evil were divided only by night and day, by the space between a respectable front door and a back door, 'blistered and distained'.[4] In the opening section of the novella, Richard Enfield, 'the well-known man about town' (p. 29), shows just how easily class boundaries, and measures of respectability, are transgressed, when he first encounters Hyde as he 'was coming home from some place at the end of the world, about three o'clock of a black winter morning' (p. 31). Soon the deserted street erupts into life as Hyde's violence awakens a spirit of repulsion which turns the women who assemble to reproach him into harpies: a single moment conjures up a world of violence, revulsion and terror. The whole novella rests upon the walks which demonstrate London's permeability, from the cherished Sunday strolls of Enfield and the lawyer Utterson, and the ill-timed night-time excursion of Danvers Carew, to Hyde's Juggernaut-like tramping through the city.

However, the main conceit of the novel obviously rests in its exploration of the divided personality and impulses of Dr Jekyll who, 'wild when he was young' (p. 41), is unable entirely to throw over that impulse to be dissolute even when appearing to be most upright. As Elaine Showalter points out, Stevenson was working in tandem with contemporary psychological research into divided personalities in drawing Jekyll, and was exploiting the most modern apprehensions of the newly complicated understanding of the workings of the unconscious in drawing his sketch of one unable success-fully to sustain the connotations of his professional persona in his personal life.[5] The fetishization by film-makers of the details of the chemical experi-ments by which Jekyll first becomes Hyde protects the viewer against the full implications of the novella in employing the trope of the mad scientist, but it is clearly the impulses in Jekyll's own personality which are the cata-lyst for his alembic ventures. The gap between vice and virtue, between the respectable professional and the dissolute Hyde, are as porous as that between the East and West Ends.

Julia Wedgwood, one of the novella's earliest critics, wrote of it as a 'remarkable work', which was concerned to investigate 'the meaning of the word *self*', which she sees as replacing the more usual fictional interest in 'the relation between man and woman'.[6] Women scarcely feature in the story at all, except as servants or women of the street, but this is not to say that what might be deemed 'the feminine' is not present. Despite his aggressively male violence, Hyde is also small, nervous, and given to fits of hysterics, all characteristics more usually culturally feminine. In the absence of women, Stevenson is liberated to discover the feminine in his male characters, and to explore the connotations of an all-male social, profes-sional, and sexual world. As the fragments of the narrative pass through the hands of lawyers and doctors, they take on a language and a set of coded references which have been associated with the hidden world of homo-sexuality underlying late-Victorian male institutions. References to left hands, to back doors, to Queer Street, to Hyde's lack of a 'namable mal-formation' (p. 40), and to blackmail (in the wake of the Labouchère Amendment, which was expected to prove a blackmailers' charter) all involve the story in the emergent explorations of homosexuality and androgyny which would dominate the 1890s. Psychologically and geo-graphically, London has become a city of doubles, of pairings and oppositions lacking their usual grounding in the male–female dyad, and exposed instead to the chaos of new social and sexual configurations, and a literature which was determined on the whole to explore, rather than to solve or to contain, such complexities.

In *New Grub Street* (1891), George Gissing's struggling writers are themselves subject to the same crossing of boundaries experienced by Stevenson's narrators and characters. In this case, however, it is the desire to be true to his vision of literature which means that Edwin Reardon is consigned to live in the slums of London along with his friend Harold Biffen, while the more market-oriented Jasper Milvain ends the novel in prosperity, and married to Reardon's widow. Class and virtue no longer determine where one might live, except in seeming to work in inverse proportion to ideas of deserving. The 'new' Grub Street of the title combines with the traditional connotations of literary hack-work associated meanings of 'grubbing' as demeaning work, of 'grub' as food. But it is unclear finally where new Grub Street is located, whether in the slums with Reardon, who is forced to grub for his food, or in respectability with Milvain, whose success is won by pandering to the lowest appetites for reading among the newly literate population. While other characters of the 1890s, such as Grant Allen's Herminia Barton (in *The Woman Who Did* (1895)), opt to live in the slums as a mark of solidarity with the working classes, they nonetheless retain their class status. Not so Gissing's writers, who find themselves ground down, and eventually are killed, by their descent into poverty.

In 1887, however, a figure emerged who would help to control, and to make comfortingly explicable, life in the city. Arthur Conan Doyle's Sherlock Holmes first appeared in *A Study in Scarlet* (1887), and achieved his greatest popularity in the short stories which appeared in the middle-brow *Strand* magazine in the 1890s. From his base at 221b Baker Street, Holmes exercised his logic in foiling criminal acts which were often set in precisely invoked London scenes. In texts which were dominated by their male leads, Holmes and the faithful Dr Watson, Conan Doyle reassures readers for whom the criminal was becoming a more pervasive category. Alongside efforts to categorize the criminal according to physiology, which were pioneered by the Italian scientist Cesare Lombroso in his *L'uomo delinquente* (1876), the 1890s were subject to fears that the criminal instinct was in fact both more pervasive and part of a general degenerative tendency, and potentially linked with the tendency to genius. As Max Nordau wrote in the dedication (to Lombroso) of his *Degeneration* (1895; originally published as *Entartung* in 1893), 'Degenerates are not always criminals, prostitutes, anarchists, and pronounced lunatics; they are often authors and artists'.[7] A figure was needed to negotiate the new configurations of the 1890s, and to insulate the reader from those fears of degeneration and decadence which were infecting society in every aspect. Holmes was such a man.

A similar figure is seen in the person of Professor van Helsing in Bram Stoker's *Dracula*, who uses his medical powers, his logic, and a knowledge of the arcane world of the supernatural and folklore to counter the presence of Dracula in London. *Dracula* was one of the best-selling novels of the decade, indeed of the century, perhaps because it thrillingly allowed readers to encounter many of the threats currently being faced by society, within a popular fantastical setting which was safeguarded by van Helsing. Dracula's sexual penetration of young women and his threat to penetrate Jonathan Harker with his teeth, his awakening of a ravening sexuality in Lucy Westenra, and the circulation of blood which his vampirism entails all bred off current fears of women's untamed sexuality which had been articulated by some new woman writers, of the new awareness of homosexuality, and of diseases such as syphilis which were passed on through sexual acts, through exchanges of fluids, and for which there was at the time no cure. Stoker's is a highly conservative novel in its attitudes to women, but highly reassuring ultimately, as it expels Dracula from London and finally sees him killed.

Decadence, disease and degeneration

The heightening of tension when it becomes known that Dracula's ultimate target is London is palpable, partly because the novel seems to suggest that the city is somehow an appropriate place for Dracula, that something in the condition of the city makes it an apt place for vampirism and the decadence which Dracula displays. In the 1880s and the 1890s, as I have begun to suggest above, the very cities which had been the scene of some of the most notable achievements of the nineteenth century seemed actively to spawn the factors contributing to its decline. In 'Fiction – Fair and Foul' (1880), John Ruskin writes of the:

> disgrace and grief resulting from the mere trampling pressure and electric friction of town life, [which] become to the sufferers peculiarly mysterious in their undeservedness, and frightful in their inevitableness. The power of all surroundings over them for evil . . . brings every law of healthy existence into question with them, and every alleged method of help and hope into doubt.[8]

Expelled as they were from the countryside, he continues, it might have been thought that, for the city's inhabitants:

he dreariness of the street would have been gilded by dreams of pastoral felicity ... but the thoroughly trained Londoner can enjoy no other excitement than that to which he has been accustomed, but asks for *that* in continually more ardent forms or more virulent concentration.

(p. 945)

The city had warped both moral and artistic sensibilities, and blunted them respectively through the sheer undiscriminating mechanics of city life and the over-stimulation which bred an ever more virulent appetite for excitement. As Shearer West notes, 'writers claimed that the development of cities had raced ahead of the ability of modern man to adapt. In attempting to adapt to such overwhelming and adverse social conditions, human beings were wearing themselves out'.[9]

In 1894, Hugh Percy Dunn was just one of a number of commentators asking 'Is Our Race Degenerating?' Dunn was relatively complacent in his answer, seeing in the increasing stature and longevity of Britons a testimony to improved medical conditions and practices developed during the previous century, and in the 'much-abused English climate' an imperative to energetic pursuits.[10] In the cricket matches which take over metropolitan parks on Saturday afternoons, and the new pursuit of cycling ('a safety-valve for reserve energy'), Dunn sees irrefutable evidence of the instinct to 'indulge in healthy, manly exercise whenever the opportunity offers' (p. 304), which is the safeguard of the nation, and which obviates the need to look to the example of Rome and the decline of *its* Empire, which, as he notes, was developing into something of a tic in nervous, pessimistic 1890s Britain. Dunn's is, however, an unusually sanguine voice in a period concerned to find an explanation for what some perceived as a continuing decline into a state of degeneration. Max Nordau's treatise suggested that physiological decline lay at the root of the moral and artistic miasma of the period, arguing for instance that the Impressionist painters developed their characteristic style not because of their efforts to capture the play of light on represented objects, but because their eyes were actually diseased and their paintings represented the state of their vision.

The threat of disease, whether actual or metaphorical, lies at the heart of fears of national degeneration, the physical symptoms working as a synecdoche for broader evidence of decay and decline in morality, art, and the economic well-being of the nation. Darwin's still potent analysis of the inter-species struggle for survival loomed darkly over a nation continuing to be beset by anxieties over the relatively more proficient economic performances of its international rivals; which was experiencing a heavy burden of increasing responsibilities in its sometimes harassing colonial possessions; and which was domestically troubled by the demands of Ireland for Home Rule, and of women for the suffrage. Within these contexts of perceived decline the advent of a new form of French-inspired literature, popularly termed 'decadent', seemed to confirm fears of a nation in decline. What for its practitioners was an exhilarating engagement with the 'new' was for its detractors evidence of decay, of a falling away from old standards which generated panicky and even hysterically totalizing reactions. Hubert Crackanthorpe wrote, in 1894, 'Decadence, decadence, you are all decadent nowadays. Ibsen, Degas, and the New English Art Club; Zola, Oscar Wilde, and the Second Mrs Tanqueray', thus sardonically exposing in his choice of references how the self-professed 'Philistines' created out of the 'new' a misleadingly homogenized target for their criticism.[11]

In his famous definition, the poet and critic Arthur Symons writes of decadent literature as having:

> all the qualities that mark the end of great periods, the qualities that we find in the Greek, the Latin, decadence; an intense self-consciousness, a restless curiosity in research, an over-subtilising refinement upon refinement, a spiritual and moral perversity. If what we call the classic is indeed the supreme art – those qualities of perfect simplicity, perfect sanity, perfect proportion, the supreme qualities – then this representative literature of to-day, interesting, beautiful, novel as it is, is really a new and beautiful and interesting disease.[12]

This deliberately provocative description perfectly captures the essence of the new literature, which was concerned to explore and to manipulate, rather than simply to describe, events, and which took as its canvas not the panoramic social settings of the earlier Victorian novel, nor the intrigues of domesticity and romance, but rather the interstices of the individual psyche as it experiences its world, devoid of many of the conditioning practices and moralities of the earlier part of the period. The experienced moment was all, as Walter Pater had expressed in the conclusion to *The Renaissance* (1873):

> our one chance is in . . . getting as many pulsations as possible into the given time. High passions may give one this quickened sense of life, ecstasy and sorrow of love, political or religious enthusiasm, or 'the enthusiasm of humanity'. Only, be sure it is passion, that it does yield you this fruit of a quickened, multiplied consciousness. Of this wisdom, the poetic passion, the desire of beauty, the love of art for art's sake, has most.[13]

So controversial was this teaching that the conclusion was suppressed in editions of 1877 and 1888, and was restored in slightly altered form in the edition of 1893, when a new audience for Pater's decadence had come into being.

The archetypal fictional British decadent hero was Dorian Gray, created by Oscar Wilde, himself still the best-known of the dandies and decadents who inhabit the popular mental map of the 1890s. Perhaps more than at any other time in the century, the gap between the real and the fictional was almost dissolved in the 1890s, so that responses to Wilde conditioned the reading of his fiction and vice versa. This elision was to prove literally fatal to Wilde, as he himself perhaps ironically recognized as he quoted from his novel when being prosecuted for obscene acts in 1895. The novel knowingly encapsulates both the essence of British decadentism and the nature of the opposition to it, and, like most of Wilde's works, may ultimately be read as a profoundly moral piece of writing, despite his suggesting in his preface that 'There is no such thing as a moral or an immoral book. Books are well written or badly written. That is all.'[14] The paradoxes which make up the text's preface recall those of Friedrich Nietzsche's *Beyond Good and Evil* (1886), where he wrote 'There are no moral phenomena at all, only a moral interpretation of phenomena' (quoted in West, p. 18). In its preoccupations and its influences then, *The Picture of Dorian Gray* also imports into Britain a form of expression and experience once believed to be safely held at bay across the Channel: its cosmopolitan character simultaneously part of decadence's danger and attractiveness.

Encouraged by the revelations of Lord Henry Wotton's personal philosophy of self-fulfilment in the yielding to temptation, and enabled by the portrait which comes to carry the visible signs of his sins, Dorian Gray lives a life devoted to minute explorations of excess, with no thought for the feelings of those who feed his experiments in living. While the nature of those experiments is scarcely more than hinted at, they nonetheless result in Dorian being socially snubbed, and in his leading the kind of double life of which Stevenson wrote, which Wilde would popularize as 'Bunburying' in his best-known comedy, *The Importance of Being Earnest*, in 1895, and which would give a shape to the evidence of Wilde's homosexuality in his trials later that year. The reception of the novel was, however, most preoccupied with what Regenia Gagnier has described as Wilde's interrogation of 'the modern and Victorian dilemma between personal individuation and social good'.[15] This tension had long been the remit of the Victorian novelist, but, for much of his novel, Wilde has his hero succumb absolutely to the pull of individual satisfaction. In his final suicide gesture, however, the forces of morality and the society which Wilde had characterized throughout as an expression of hypocrisy are nonetheless allowed to triumph as the ghastliness of Dorian's sins are made manifest.

The possibility of a moral reading is, however, eschewed in contemporary responses which rather regard Dorian Gray as epitomizing that 'ego-mania' (Nordau's term) which was perceived as one of the most common and distressing symptoms of both pathological degeneration and literary decadence. From Ibsen's heroines to the young men who fell victim to the suicide cult of the 1890s, ego-mania was held to be at the root of their diseased outlook and anti-social actions.[16] The fabric of the social, which the Victorian novel had done so much both to celebrate in its pages and to confirm in its creation of a unified audience, looked set to unravel in the face of 'a new Hedonism that was to re-create life, and to save it from that harsh, uncomely puritanism that is having, in our own day, its curious revival' (*Dorian Gray*, p. 162), and in which evil became simply 'a mode through which [Dorian] could realize his conception of the beautiful' (p. 179).

In the response of the self-proclaimed Philistines to decadence, the ego became synonymous with evil as competing forms of identification and self-knowledge split audiences and communities. The Philistines are parodied in George and Weedon Grossmith's *The Diary of a Nobody* (1892) in which the Pooters' hapless son, Lupin (surely an ironic noticing of the decadents' perceived obsession with flowers), represents the worst excesses of which his father can conceive in staying out late, proposing an unsuitable marriage, and laughing at his father's friends. Lupin is no decadent, but his misdemeanours are perceived as being at one with those anti-social leanings that seemed to put personal satisfaction before the social good. Precisely what was the nature of that social good, was, indeed, being profoundly questioned at this period, as was the nature of society and the social compact. But, rather than generating this social interrogation, the decadents simply exploited the fissures it opened up, and explored the possibilities of the new configurations it envisaged. Wilde's associating with rent boys of a lower class was simply the most shocking example of this trend, combining as it did sexual and social transgressions.

For many, the Wilde trials of 1895 epitomized the nature of the decadent threat, and thus came conveniently to signal the end of the decadent movement in Britain. Later that year, Hugh E.M. Stutfield wrote crowingly of Wilde as 'our late prophet of the aesthetes', and of a perceived reaction in favour of more moderate views,[17] and Max Beerbohm recorded that he was feeling 'a trifle out-moded'.[18] The rumour that Wilde had been arrested while carrying a copy of the *Yellow Book*, the best known 'decadent' magazine (Wilde was in fact reading a French novel), was enough effectively to end the career as its art editor of Aubrey Beardsley, the foremost decadent

British artist who was parodied in *Punch*, the citadel of the Philistine, as Mortarthurio Whiskersley. Many of Beardsley's erotic and visually punning drawings, which included a series of illustrations of Wilde's *Salome*, confronted the viewer with casually invoked images of genitalia which seemed unacceptably subversive to many, especially in their unexpected combinations. The androgyne haunts Beardsley's art, as it did Wilde's history and the culture of the 1890s.

The new woman

Studies of sexual inversion, such as the first volume of Havelock Ellis's *Studies in the Psychology of Sex* (1897), gave scientific credibility to fears of the merging of sexual characteristics; the spectre of androgyny was one of the factors which enabled a link in the public's mind between the twin fears of the decadent and the 'new woman'. As we will see, this phrase is a highly flexible one, used by women's supporters and detractors alike, but necessarily carrying implicit within it a questioning of traditional female roles. To their opponents, the new women were of doubtful gender, described by Eliza Lynn Linton, keen as ever to assert her own distance from such anarchic figures, as rebellious 'Maenads', 'contemptuous of men, unloving to children,' or as lesbians.[19] She also characterizes women's 'clamour for political rights' as 'their confession of sexual enmity', seeing in such actions 'a curious inversion of sex'.[20] But, to some of the new women themselves, their actions exemplified the assertion of a form of feminine morality and purity at odds with, and otherwise unavailable within, contemporary society. The novelist and essayist Sarah Grand wrote that women were concerned to 'raise the race a step higher in the scale of being', with Mona Caird asserting that this would be achieved through a purity which 'is becoming one of the regenerative and moving forces of the century'.[21]

The 'new woman' term is primarily of use in signalling a coalescence of the variety of movements for the reform of women's situation which we have already noticed taking place through the century. Some were profoundly contradictory, such as Caird's and Grand's emphasis on purity, and other writers stressing women's sensuality, but all claimed for women the right to a full and autonomous life, and to question conventions and traditional practices. Historically, the period saw the expansion of employment opportunities for middle-class women, and the consolidation and protection of those jobs in the foundation of a women's Trade Union Association in 1889. The first woman sat on the London County Council in

1888, women became eligible for election to parish and district councils in 1894, and from 1893 could become government factory inspectors. However, despite the increase in women's social and political responsibilities, their accession to the vote seemed as far away as ever. Suffrage societies were set up throughout the country, culminating in the establishment of the National Union of Women's Suffrage Societies in 1897. In the same year a women's suffrage bill passed a second reading in the House of Commons by a majority of 228 to 157, before being defeated in the Lords, and it was not until after the First World War that any women were given the vote. Though a popular (largely middle-class) movement, it was far from being the case, however, that all women supported the suffrage agitation. In 1889, an appeal against women's suffrage, signed by around 2,000 women, appeared in the *Nineteenth Century* periodical. The signatories included many well-known women, such as the novelist Mrs Humphry Ward, but even such a retrograde action was itself of course proof of women's inherent capacity for and interest in politics, and fuelled the debate which the signatories had sought to quell.

The question of the vote struck at more fundamental issues even than employment, education, and property reforms. If it could be envisaged that a woman might choose to vote differently from her husband then a fundamental understanding of marriage and the family was being jeopardized:

> Where there is now, in the main, harmony and affection, would arise discussion and discord; the authority of the father would be impaired. In a word, this agitation to incorporate women in the electorate is nothing more nor less than a revolt against the male headship of the family.[22]

The challenge to the institution of marriage was a central part of the new woman's activities, and received backing from the courts in 1891, when they upheld a wife's right to resist her husband's use of force in insisting that she share the marital home.[23] Mona Caird's article on 'Marriage' in the *Westminster Review* of 1888 analysed the custom as one based in a capitalist ethos and in men's monopolizing jealousy, and hence necessarily unpropitious for the survival of love and good feeling. She advocated instead a form of free marriage based solely on the continuance of the desire to be together. The *Daily Telegraph* took up the issue, inviting its readers to contribute letters to a column entitled 'Is Marriage a Failure?' In all, around 27,000 letters were received, thus, as Sally Ledger notes, extending the debate on marriage far beyond the ranks of the new woman and the radical readers of the *Westminster Review*.[24] Even the Pooters are made aware of the furore:

NOVEMBER 2. I spent the evening quietly with Carrie, of whose company I never tire. We had a most pleasant chat about the letters on 'Is Marriage a Failure?' It has been no failure in our case. In talking over our own happy experiences, we never noticed that it was past midnight.[25]

As new freedoms were achieved by women, it seemed to many that to marry would be to deny oneself that newly won autonomy. As the novelist Ella Hepworth Dixon wrote in 1899:

If young and pleasing women are permitted to go to college, to live alone, to travel, to have a profession, to belong to a club, to give parties, to read and discuss whatsoever seems good to them, and to go to theatres without masculine escort they have most of the privileges – and several others thrown in – for which the girl of 20 or 30 years ago was ready to barter herself to the first suitor who offered himself and the shelter of his name. Then again, a capable woman who has begun a career and feels certain of advancement in it, is often as shy of entangling herself matrimonially as ambitious young men have ever shown themselves under like circumstances.[26]

Like Caird, Grand, and Dixon, many of the contributors to the new woman debate were novelists as well as essayists and critics, and it was in their fiction that they achieved both most notoriety and most polemical success. In their hands, the novel became not simply a campaigning tool, but the actual vehicle of change. The new woman novelist took the novel, long acknowledged as the most appropriate literary form for women, and the domestic subject-matter for which they were most renowned, and combined them to produce a new school of politically motivated fiction which exposed women's anger and frustration at the conditions in which they lived and, by incursions into fantasy, envisaged a more utopian future. These novels were perhaps most successful in converting the matter of autobiography, which was freely drawn on, into representative narratives with which all women might identify. This act of calling upon, and constructing, a common readership through empathetic reading practices was the hallmark of the new woman novelist's work, and also the source of her power to disturb.

This empathetic aesthetic had been fostered first in the theatre, where the new woman character was an integral part of the experiments with the so-called 'new drama', which was displacing English farces and drawing-room comedies. In 1889, Ibsen's *A Doll's House* (written in 1879) was produced in London by Charles Charrington and his wife Janet Achurch, who played

Ibsen's heroine Nora. The play created uproar with its tale of a young wife, a doll in her own house, who eventually realizes her predicament, and in coming swiftly to maturity decides to leave her husband and children for the sake of her own well-being and development as an individual. Nora justifies her decision in part as one made for the children too, who should not be brought up by one who could not be a good example to them, but nonetheless her decision was widely abused. The influential theatre critic Clement Scott writes ironically of how Nora creates a new 'ideal':

> It is all self, self, self! This is the ideal woman of the new creed . . . not the pattern woman we have admired in our mothers and our sisters, not the model of unselfishness and charity, but a mass of aggregate conceit and self-sufficiency, who leaves her home and deserts her friendless children because she has *herself* to look after.[27]

Yet, for a group of women who went to see the play together, thus exercising those new freedoms of which Dixon wrote, the play was a revelation. Edith Lees, later Mrs Havelock Ellis, writes of how she and a group of friends, including Olive Schreiner, Eleanor Marx, and Mrs Holman Hunt, were left at the end of the play:

> restive and impetuous and almost savage in our arguments. This was either the end of the world or the beginning of the new world for women. What did it mean? Was there hope or despair in the banging of that door [as Nora leaves home]? Was it life or death for women? Was it joy or sorrow for men? Was it revelation or disaster? We almost cantered home.[28]

The women come together as a new form of audience, all-female and politically excited by what they see, and thus prefigure both women's response to new woman fiction and their political activities in the 1890s.

Ella Hepworth Dixon's *The Story of a Modern Woman* (1894) tells the history of Mary Erle, daughter of loving parents, both of whom die early, and leave Mary to fend for herself, and to support her younger and rather feckless brother. It tells of her useless attempts to turn a young lady's accomplishments in art into a career, of how her lack of money loses her a fiancé, and of the minute humiliations and drudgeries of middle-class poverty, in this case generated by a lack of preparation for an independent life. As such the novel is a fascinating document of contemporary life, but it gains its political impact by the parallel narrative of Mary Erle's friend, Alison Ives, who discovers her doctor-fiancé to have been responsible for the seduction, ruin, and death of a young woman from the country whom Alison befriends. As Alison lies dying she enjoins upon Mary the importance

of women's loyalty to each other, and of the potential strength of such stead-
fastness:

> 'Promise me that you will never, never do anything to hurt another
> woman,' said the sick girl, running her finger along the pattern on the
> counterpane. 'I don't suppose for an instant you ever would. But there
> come times in our lives when we can do a great deal of good, or an
> incalculable amount of harm. If women only used their power in the
> right way! If we were only united we could lead the world.'[29]

The essence of the new woman's fiction rests in the possibility that it can act
to shift the centre of gravity in contemporary society away from male-led
decisions, so that women have at least an equal if not a more prominent role
in leading society. The coalescing of women in a self-conscious political
body is an integral part of this process.

Women's fiction of the 1890s explored with frankness the new opportunities offered by their access to work and education. But it also experimented with the representation of a newly autonomous form of female
sexuality and desire, which came to be regarded as the most intimate and
outrageous assault on the status quo. Some critics responded with predict-
able and disproportionate outrage to the new woman's writing of sex. Mrs
Oliphant wrote that women's struggles had resulted in their selection of 'one
small fact of life' as the most important thing in existence, and that 'I do not
choose to sully my lips with the name which the lower passion thus selected
bears, and it is painful to me, a woman, to refer to it'.[30] J.A. Noble wrote
that 'one colossal appetite' dominated the new fictions of sexuality, that 'the
sexual passion provides the main-spring of their action, and within its range
lies their whole gamut of emotion'.[31] In fact, relatively little of the new
woman writer's output is concerned with sex, and, when it is, the central
focus is often rather on its dangers than its pleasures. Sarah Grand's *The
Heavenly Twins* (1893) was one of the most notorious novels of the decade
in this respect, but its concern is rather with female sexual ignorance and the
dangers of a sexual double standard which can visit upon a young wife and
her child the horrors of hereditary syphilis. Likewise, the short stories of
George Egerton, which appeared in the collections *Keynotes* (1893) and
Discords (1894), and which Noble regards as 'merely or mainly conduits of
sexual emotion' (p. 494), are often fables of female effort and co-operation.
'A Cross Line' was perhaps Egerton's most famous and notorious story, and
featured a whisky-drinking, fly-fishing heroine. Though tempted by the
anonymous man in grey with whom she fishes, her only moment of passion
in the story is experienced with her husband who 'crushes her soft little
body to him and carries her off to her room'.[32] However, it is perhaps in her

fantasies that Egerton's heroine most offends, as she dreams of subduing stadia of men by her intoxicating dancing, by her expression of that 'eternal wildness, the untamed primitive savage temperament' that she dangerously suggests is lurking 'in the mildest, best woman' (p. 267). The story ends with the heroine's pregnancy and her decision to stay with her husband rather than run away to the man in grey. More importantly, it ends with the heroine's and her maid's moment of communion over a box of baby clothes and a lock of hair which the maid has saved since the death of her illegitimate baby. This cross-class communication is the story's most potent moment, and yet predictably it is her smoking, fishing, and direct way of speaking that *Punch* parodies in 'She-Notes' by Borgia Smudgiton.

It is far easier to parody as eccentric or coarse a new form of expression than to seek to realize the reconfiguring of power which underlies it. Some male novelists employed the figure of the new woman in their art as a figure of curiosity and novelty, and entirely failed to engage with the dimensions of her politics. In *The Woman Who Did*, Grant Allen frames his free-thinking heroine within a discourse redolent with old values. She enters upon her free union with Alan Merrick, the father of her child, dressed in a virginal white robe, which makes her either a victim or one who is unconsciously aping a marriage ceremony in what Allen presents as an atavistic instinct to conform, and one which Herminia ignores at her peril. She finally dies by her own hand, when she realizes that her daughter Dolores has not become the new and free woman she hoped for, but one who yearns for the shows of respectability her mother repudiated. Herminia dies so as not to stand in the way of Dolores' marriage, and thus Allen has her admit the new woman's defeat, and enact the limitation of her ends. A new woman author, like Dixon or Grand, would rather have had her heroine live to fight her battles.

The year 1895 sees something of a watershed in the fortunes of new woman fiction. Elided with the decadent in their critics' eyes, both groups suffered through the fall of Oscar Wilde. However, such an elision requires a substantial critical sleight of hand. Read apart from their political context and motivations, the new woman's concern with sexual experience could become simply another form of the decadent experimentation with representations of sensuality. But, in fact, the new woman writer's interests could scarcely be further removed from those of the decadent. The new woman writer was concerned to write to effect change: hers was a profoundly moral and political art, and could not be divorced from the other contexts which she and her art inhabited. Also, while the decadent did nothing to dispel fears of degeneration, the new woman repudiated the Darwin-inspired gloom of a descent into evolutionary darkness by concentrating on trying to remedy problems. (See extract 4, p. 140.) Vernon Lee wrote in 1896 of the way in which Nordau's concentration on 'merely physiological disturbances' acts to divert 'attention from what I should call sociological causes of deterioration, namely, the undue pressure on the individual of social habits, routines, and institutions'.[33] In a curious alliance, the decadents, with their emphasis on the moment of experience, and Nordau act together to facilitate the degenerative despondency which the new woman, for all her justified pessimism, resisted.

The end of the novel?

Nordau and his followers feared decadence as a herald of the end of European civilization. In Britain that fear had a particular resonance as the state of the British Empire came to seem more imperilled. Mindful of the decline into decadence of the once all-powerful Roman Empire, some elements of British society were quick to point to the aesthetes as heralding the end of Britain's sway in the world. As the 1890s progressed it became clear that Britain could not indeed maintain its position of world dominance unchallenged. Quite apart from the threat of foreign traders competing for space within the Empire, the countries of the Empire themselves were not as stable and loyal as might have been hoped.

In India, the founding of the Indian National Congress in December 1885 marked the beginning of attempts to consolidate a national Indian identity, in the face of British rule. In the first instance, however, the Congress was taken less than seriously, and, as Ronald Hyam writes, 'Between 1886 and 1892 the British aim in respect of Congress was to forestall radical nationalist demands by offering timely concessions'.[34] The political system of which Congress was the centre had importantly enabled some degree of elected political representation to be a possibility in India. However, this meant that the maintenance of British rule might simply become even more unpalatable, especially under such viceroys as Curzon (1899–1902), who spoke of Indians as 'less than schoolchildren' and of Congress as failing to represent, or even to interest, the bulk of Indians whom he believed to be an illiterate, politically uninformed race (Hyam, *Britain's Imperial Century*, pp. 184–5). As the twentieth century was to show, however, the Congress was simply the first stage in the inexorable move towards independence for India, which was achieved in 1948.

The best-known late-Victorian author of Indian tales and novels was Rudyard Kipling, whose *Plain Tales from the Hills* appeared in 1888 and

The Jungle Book in 1894. The *Plain Tales*, which first appeared in the *Civil and Military Gazette*, are interesting in suggesting that India is both strangely immaterial and absolutely fathomable to Kipling's military characters in their camps and their expatriate society. The police officer Strickland, in 'Miss Youghal's Sais', goes native and penetrates the Indian caste system, moving at ease among servants and Englishmen. India is often perversely irrelevant to short stories whose terms and preoccupations rather signal the anxieties of domestic English culture than the responsibilities of the colonial power, and becomes simply a backdrop before which perversities and limitations may be more freely expressed and more readily resolved. Effeminate young officers, like 'the Boy' in 'Thrown Away', might meet their deaths in remote outposts, and have their deaths more easily hushed up, or find a space for cross-dressing jokes (in 'His Wedded Wife') which are neutralized by their military context. Marital brutality can be invoked as a curiosity and summarily dealt with by a horse-whipping (in 'The Bronckhorst Divorce-Case') which, it is implied, is a form of natural justice no longer easily available in England. India exists only in so far as the narrative of English-ness demands it as a foil.

It was arguably, however, in Africa that the greatest challenge to the Empire was felt, and that the signs of the eventual end of the Empire and indeed of the desire to maintain an Empire began to be perceived.[35] The strategic significance of South Africa was clear, given the importance of the Cape route for British trading ships. It was also a country rich in mineral resources and in opportunities for British capitalists. However, the stability of the region in the 1890s was in question. Following the discovery of a major gold field in the Transvaal in 1886, power and influence moved away from the British Cape to the Afrikaner-dominated Transvaal. Given German support for the Afrikaners, this development threatened serious repercussions for British rule. Technically, the Transvaal was forbidden to undertake negotiations with foreign powers without Britain's approval, but the immigration by Germans into the area, and their subsequent substantial investment in the Transvaal, meant that their presence was strongly felt. The situation was further worsened by the doomed 'Jameson raid' into the Transvaal carried out by Dr Leander Starr Jameson, in the hope of recapturing the area for British influence. The raid went disastrously wrong, however, with Jameson surrendering to the Boers four days after beginning his assault. Arguably the most important result of the raid was to heighten Boer suspicion, if not outright hatred, of the British, and thus to prepare the way for the beginning of the Anglo-Boer War in 1899.

The onset of war seems to have been more carefully negotiated than is perhaps usually the case, with a degree of cynicism and an eye on the importance of popular opinion back in Britain governing discussions. The war was deemed necessary in order to ensure that the British not the Dutch were in control of South Africa, but there was reluctance on the British part to seem to be the aggressor, hence there was much relief when the war began on the pretext of a Boer ultimatum. Local grievances were exploited in justifying Britain's desire to take control of a situation in which national prestige seemed to be at stake, and hence, potentially, Britain's influence in other of its colonial outposts too. The end of the war, as expressed by the then Governor of South Africa, Sir Alfred Milner, was the achievement of 'a self-governing white community, supported by a well treated and justly governed black labour force from Cape Town to Zambesia' (quoted in Hyam, *Britain's Imperial Century*, p. 245). Content to use black labour for its own ends during the war, Britain did not materially benefit that group following its eventual victory. After two and a half years of fighting, the Boers surrendered, leaving Britain in control, but, as after the Crimea victory, counting the costs of victory rather than enjoying its spoils. Weaknesses in the British military had again been revealed, and questions had been raised about some of its strategies, including the now notorious practice of 'concentrating' Boer women and children in camps, which was described by the Liberal leader Sir Henry Campbell-Bannerman in 1901 as barbaric.[36] An estimated 26,000 women and children died in the poorly run camps. It was such events as these that perhaps, as Porter suggests, 'exhausted the imperial enthusiasm of the British people' (p. 181).

In the war and its aftermath, they encountered colonialism's dark side, its less than grand and patriotic nature, its basis in commerce and competitive capitalism, and the human costs of its perpetuation. Also in 1899, Joseph Conrad published 'Heart of Darkness' as a short serial in *Blackwood's Magazine*. Its being placed thus in the very heart of the world of British publishing is crucial to its meaning and its first readers, as it, too, forcibly acts out the brutality of the colonialist project. Though ostensibly concerned with the Belgian Congo, and not with British Africa, the experiences of which Conrad's narrator Marlow tells might apply to the whole continent. Despite his assertion that in the 'red' parts of the map, denoting British control, 'some real work is being done', nonetheless we also have to recognize that London and British trade are implicated in the setting of the story on board a boat lying in the Thames estuary, with the 'mournful gloom' of the sky 'brooding motionless over the biggest, and the greatest, town on earth'.[37] As he goes on, 'What greatness had not floated on the ebb of that river into the mystery of an unknown earth! . . . The dreams of men, the seed of commonwealths, the germs of empires' (p. 47). The twilight deepens around Marlow and his hearers as the atmosphere thickens and darkens in his story, and he approaches nearer to his meeting with Kurtz, the renowned ivory trader.

Before Marlow encounters the horrors of Kurtz's experience, he is exposed to the indigenous suffering caused by white trading, and to the grotesqueness of the efforts needed to support that trade. Soldiers travelling to protect national interests in Africa drown in the surf, as they disembark from a ship, and others shell the bush from their boat (pp. 60–1). As Conrad writes, there is something disconcertingly insane, lugubriously droll, and altogether disorientating about such actions. Edward Said suggests that: 'By accentuating the discrepancy between the official "idea" of empire and the remarkably disorientating actuality of Africa, Marlow unsettles the reader's sense not only of the very idea of empire but of something more basic, reality itself.'[38] Most horrific of all, however, is Marlow's attempt to take a refreshing walk in the shade of some trees. It soon becomes clear, as he notes, that he 'had stepped into the gloomy circle of some Inferno', where black workers had come to die:

> Near the same tree two more bundles of acute angles sat with their legs drawn up. . . . While I stood horror-struck, one of these creatures rose on his hands and knees, and went off on all-fours towards the river to drink. He lapped out of his hand, then sat up in the sunlight, crossing his shins in front of him, and after a time let his woolly head fall on his breastbone.
>
> (p. 67)

After such an encounter, almost any attempt to carry on takes on something of the ludicrousness of the soldiers firing into the bush.

As the optimism of the colonial experience was interrogated by Conrad and the Boer War, so also was the place of Britain's colonial status in the make-up of both the nation's and the individual's self-professed identity. Kurtz's encounter with the darkness of Africa propels another journey into the darkness of his own being, from which there is no return, and which the novelist struggles to convey in the narrative form available to him. The concept of identity is rendered peculiarly vulnerable by the journey taken by Kurtz and arguably by Marlow too. This vulnerability far exceeds the challenges to masculinity being encountered during the 1890s, and even, as Tim Middleton suggests, challenges the capacity of narrative to convey its dimensions: 'the truth which Kurtz glimpses cannot be transposed into the period's categories'.[39] In particular, Conrad and Marlow struggle with the being of Kurtz, with the sensation of knowing him: 'Do you see him? Do you see the story? Do you see anything?', and fall back in knowing dissatisfaction on the language of dreaming which becomes inadequate as soon as it is employed, for 'no relation of a dream can convey the dream-sensation, that commingling of absurdity, surprise, and bewilderment in a tremor of struggling revolt, that notion of being captured by the incredible which is of the very essence of dreams' (p. 82).

Within 'Heart of Darkness' the dissolving of a knowable identity works alongside the fragmentation of narrative and the exposure of the horrors of colonialism to constitute a text which acts out the fundamental fears of endings with which the 1890s were beset, and which demonstrates how essential to the concept of identity was the capacity of narrative to tell and re-tell that identity, and of institutions to support that identity. As both narrative and institution were routinely brought into question in the *fin de siècle*, so too was the individual at their centre.

Of no novel is this more true than Hardy's *Jude the Obscure* (1895), which pits the individual against the forces of religion (experienced as a man-made institution in the novel), of education, and of a morality which is based on social expediency. In his three best-known late novels, *Jude, The Mayor of Casterbridge* (1886), and *Tess of the D'Urbervilles* (1891), Hardy sets the tales of his main protagonists' tragic deaths in a context of the decline of the rural way of life, which was precipitated by the intervention of both an inexorable fate and a system of social expectations based rather on town than country needs. As Hardy writes of Tess after her fall:

> she looked upon herself as a figure of Guilt intruding into the haunts of innocence. But all the while she was making a distinction where there was no difference. Feeling herself in antagonism she was quite in accord. She had been made to break an accepted social law, but no law known to the environment in which she fancied herself such an anomaly.[40]

Tess generated controversy with its sub-title, 'A Pure Woman', which was seen as highly controversial when applied to the story of a milk-maid seduced or perhaps raped by a man posing as her wealthy cousin. It also courted accusations of blasphemy in its scene of Tess baptizing her dying baby, when her father refuses to allow a parson into his house to perform the task.

Undaunted by criticism which must have seemed rather to prove the point of his novel, Hardy returned to issues of purity and belief in *Jude the Obscure*, and his study of the aspirations and marriages of Jude Fawley and his cousin Sue Bridehead. The story of Jude is in part that of 'the modern vice of unrest'.[41] Jude is condemned by his scholarly aspirations, fuelled by the dream-like vision of Christminster across the fields, and a young crush on the schoolmaster Phillotson, to a peripatetic life, spent trying to move away from his home village of Marygreen, and from the class of labourers to which he belongs. Obtaining employment as a stonemason in

Christminster, as a first means of entering the city, Jude has what Hardy describes as a moment of 'true illumination; that here in the stone yard was a centre of effort as worthy as that dignified by the name of scholarly study within the noblest of the colleges. But he lost it under stress of his old idea' (p. 131) about learning. The novel is set in the 1860s. By the 1890s, a variety of university extension schemes were in operation to help men and women like Jude who, because of their lack of resources, could not yet hope to attend university regularly.

However, the novel also deals with a more intractable problem standing in Jude's way, and one which was of central interest to his first readers. Jude is first diverted from his studies by his desire for Arabella, a coarse country-woman who attracts Jude's attention by throwing a pig's penis at him. Entrapped into marriage by Arabella pretending to be pregnant, Jude finds:

> something wrong in a social ritual which made necessary a cancelling of well-formed schemes involving years of thought and labour, of fore-going a man's one opportunity of showing himself superior to the lower animals, and of contributing his units of work to the general progress of his generation, because of a momentary surprise by a new and transitory instinct which had nothing in it of the nature of vice, and could only be at the most called weakness.
>
> (p. 107, pt. 1, ch. 9)

Though stressing in the face of outraged reviews that he had not intended to write a problem novel in the vein of others of the time which concerned marriage, *Jude* was nonetheless reviewed and read in the context of other 'anti-marriage' texts, with this gloss determining also readings of Jude's relationship with Sue Bridehead. Mrs Oliphant was the most outspoken of the many critics who read the novel in this way, writing of the offence of Hardy's depictions of Arabella ('a human pig'), and of Sue as one 'who makes virtue vicious by keeping the physical facts of one relationship in life in constant prominence by denying, as Arabella does by satisfying them'.[42]

The review rather struggles to sustain this reading, and has necessarily to ignore much of the novel, but it was not untypical of responses which sought to map the novel by familiar co-ordinates. In this respect, it also comes as no surprise to find the rhetoric of decadence invading even more favourable reviews, such as that of Edmund Gosse, who writes of Jude as 'a neurotic subject in whom neurotic degeneracy takes an idealist turn', and of Sue as 'a poor, maimed degenerate, ignorant of herself and of the perversion of her instincts'.[43] In their recourse to a common language of denigration and categorization, critics failed to grasp the larger issues which Hardy invoked, and which he described as 'a deadly war waged between flesh and spirit ... [and] the tragedy of unfulfilled aims' in his preface to the first volume edition of the novel (p. 39). As he was to write 16 years later, in a postscript to his preface, 'the greater part of the story – that which presented the shattered ideals of the two chief characters, and had been more especially, and indeed almost exclusively, the part of interest to myself – was practically ignored by the adverse press' in both Britain and America (p. 40). In some respects, this is because the reasons for the shattering of Sue's and Jude's ideals are too overwhelming, and their consequences too serious to be fully envisaged in a period already beset by more local difficulties.

As the novel develops and its focus shifts to include Sue as well as Jude, the irreconcilabilities of individual instinct and religion pale in comparison with the incompatibilities in evidence between Jude and Sue, characters who have a perfect reciprocity between them (p. 263, pt. 4, ch. 1), who are described by Phillotson as 'almost the two parts of a single whole' (p. 361, pt. 5, ch. 5), yet whose love is impossible for reasons other than those of the religious and social customs governing marriage and divorce. In Sue, who according to George Egerton is of 'a temperament less rare than the ordinary male observer supposes',[44] we find a woman utterly at odds with the implications of her femaleness, and who enters only under duress, and the strain of her jealousy of Arabella, into sexual relations with Jude. As Jude aspires to be a scholar, so does she aspire to live a life of a more intellectual and spiritual communion with a man. She is repeatedly described as ethereal, gossamer-like, as she tries to evade the implications of the flesh which have so beset other women. In no other text of the period are the contemporary dangers and unavoidable limitations of the sexually active female body so brutally spelt out, as Sue feels herself becoming ensnared by Jude's demands of her and by the children she bears. She tries to take recourse in what she describes as a return to instincts, to 'Greek joyousness' which can forget 'what twenty-five centuries have taught the race since their time' (p. 366, pt. 5, ch. 5), and which can crucially subdue the body to the mind. But she is defeated in what is fundamentally an intellectual conceit by the deaths of her children. In his study of Hardy, D.H. Lawrence writes of the tragedy of their deaths thus:

> She was glad to have children, to prove that she was a woman. But in her it was a perversity to wish to prove she was a woman. She was no woman. And her children, the proof thereof, vanished like hoar-frost from her.[45]

Lawrence's is a sympathetic, yet fundamentally estranged, reading, seeing in Sue one who was seeking to identify herself with a male principle. While this is too crude a reading of her difficulties of sexual identification, Lawrence's take on Sue's and Jude's scarcely realized children is persuasive, and high-lights the inescapable fact of children in confirming and confining women's sexuality and identity in the 1890s.

The deaths of the children and of Jude, and Sue's awful self-immuration in a re-marriage to Phillotson, are the appalling ends of their ideals, ideals wrecked not only by their unsympathetic moment in time, but also by the incompatibility of their masculine and feminine natures, and their own interpretations of those natures and of their recourse to what they describe as instinct. Jude and Sue not only fail to find a sympathetic space anywhere in their society, but also fail really to find proper sympathy in each other. It is not true to say, as Arabella does with the easy complacency of popular fiction, that Sue 'has never found peace since she left [Jude's] arms, and never will again till she's as he is now!' (p. 491, pt. 6, ch. 11). She never found lasting peace even with Jude. This absolute irreconcilability between man and woman, allied to the suicides which provide the effective endings for all of the main characters – for Jude and Sue commit suicide as surely as did Old Father Time – makes the novel the fulfilment of the worst fears abroad in the 1890s, but also exceeds those fears by taking the grounds of them into new dimensions to which solutions are not immediately apparent. Not only is the state of marriage flawed, but men and women might actually be fundamentally incompatible in that relationship. No wonder then that his critics sought to reclaim familiar territory in their reviews.

The effect of the reviews on Hardy was devastating, even for one who had faced extremely hostile criticism after the publication of *Tess*. In addition to the regular antipathy of the professional reviewers, the book was burned by the Bishop of Wakefield, who also persuaded W.H. Smith to remove *Jude* from its circulating library (Millgate, *Thomas Hardy*, p. 372). Even Gosse, Hardy's friend and sympathetic critic, could not help finding himself 'stunned with a sense of the hollowness of existence' after reading *Jude*, and surprised that Hardy was not more sensible to beauty than *Jude* seemed to show (Millgate, *Thomas Hardy*, p. 370). It was surely with some relief that Hardy now found himself sufficiently wealthy to be able to turn his back on fiction and concentrate on writing poetry for the rest of his career.

In some ways, *Jude the Obscure* also put an end to what we think of as the Victorian novel. It seems effectively to have broken a contract between the author and novelist which had managed to persist throughout the vicissitudes and unprecedented social transformation of the rest of the century. Of course, publishing practices had changed, and the novel as a material object was perhaps less venerated in the newspaper age of the 1890s than it had been previously. In a letter rebuking Gosse for finding 'grimy' features in *Jude*, Hardy explains that such elements:

go to show the contrast between the ideal life a man wished to lead, & the squalid life he was fated to lead. . . . I must have lamentably failed, as I feel I have, if this requires explanation & is not self-evident. The idea was meant to run all through the novel. It is, in fact to be discovered in *every*body's life – though it lies less on the surface perhaps than it does in my poor puppet's.

(quoted in Millgate, *Thomas Hardy*, p. 370)

Hardy's incredulity at his audience not being willing to embrace his reading of their lives is instructive. Hostility might of course denote recognition as well as denial on a reader's part, but it was surely unreasonable to expect a wholesale embracing of the squalidness that Hardy deems to be the human lot. In the novel there is a fundamental unpicking of the basis of, or the aspiration to, a domestic and familial loyalty and affection which had previously protected both protagonist and reader against the existential crisis which besets Jude, and in the face of which his final words, quoted from Job, take on the blackest irony.

After *Jude* it seems that there was scarcely anywhere for reader and novelist to turn except away from the novel, whose essence had for so long been founded in complicated and often interrogatory ways upon the domestic privacies subsisting alongside the public contexts with which this book has been dealing. Once those privacies had been shown to be fundamentally and always a sham, a form of faith in the novel was lost. The short story comes into its own at this period, enabling experimentation with utopian futures and alternative presents. The realist novel succumbs to the shorter narrative, and to the novel of fantasy and superstition, such as *Dracula* or *The Time Machine*, and that of life beyond the domestic, and beyond Britain, such as Conrad's *Lord Jim* and *The Nigger of the 'Narcissus'* (1897). Before Victoria's reign ended, then, the Victorian novel had run its course, but was, and is still, far from exhausting its fascination for readers and critics alike.

Notes

1 Quoted in Karl Beckson, *London in the 1890s: A Cultural History* (New York and London, 1992), pp. 19–20.
2 Oscar Wilde, 'The Soul of Man Under Socialism', in *Plays, Prose Writings and Poems* (London, 1996), pp. 15–47 (p. 23).
3 Judith R. Walkowitz, *City of Dreadful Delight: Narratives of Sexual Danger in Late-Victorian London* (Chicago, 1992) p. 200.
4 Robert Louis Stevenson, *Dr Jekyll and Mr Hyde and Other Stories* (Harmondsworth, 1979), p. 30.

5 See Elaine Showalter, 'Dr Jekyll's Closet', in *Sexual Anarchy: Gender and Culture at the* Fin de Siècle (London, 1990), pp. 105–26.

6 Julia Wedgwood, 'Contemporary Records: Fiction', *Contemporary Review*, 49 (1886), 590–8 (p. 594).

7 Max Nordau, *Degeneration* (London, 1895), p. vii.

8 John Ruskin, 'Fiction – Fair and Foul', *Nineteenth Century*, 7 (1880), 941–62 (p. 943).

9 Shearer West, *Fin de Siècle* (London, 1993), p. 25.

10 Hugh Percy Dunn, 'Is Our Race Degenerating?', *Nineteenth Century*, 36 (1894), 301–14 (p. 306).

11 Hubert Crackanthorpe, 'Reticence in Literature', *Yellow Book*, 2 (1894), 259–69 (p. 266). Of Crackanthorpe's references, Ibsen, Degas, Zola, and Wilde are well known. The New English Art Club was founded in 1886, in reaction against the Royal Academy. It was influenced by the French open-air painters. *The Second Mrs Tanqueray* is a play by Arthur Wing Pinero, which was first produced in London in 1893. It made a star of Mrs Patrick Campbell, who played Paula Tanqueray, a prostitute who marries well, but whose past tracks her down, and eventually prompts her to commit an honourable suicide.

12 Arthur Symons, 'The Decadent Movement in Literature' (1893), in *Dramatis Personae* (London, 1925), pp. 96–117 (p. 97).

13 Walter H. Pater, *Studies in the History of the Renaissance* (London, 1873), pp. 212–13.

14 Oscar Wilde, *The Picture of Dorian Gray* (Harmondsworth, 1985, p. 21.

15 Regenia Gagnier, 'Wilde and the Victorians', in Peter Raby, ed., *The Cambridge Companion to Oscar Wilde* (Cambridge, 1997), pp. 18–33 (p. 24).

16 For an account of the suicide-cult, see John Stokes, ' "Tired of life": Letters, Literature and the Suicide Craze', in *In the Nineties* (Hemel Hempstead, 1989), pp. 115–44.

17 Hugh E.M. Stutfield, 'Tommyrotics', *Blackwood's Edinburgh Magazine*, 157 (1895), 833–45 (p. 839).

18 Quoted in Holbrook Jackson, *The Eighteen Nineties* (London, 1913), p. 17.

19 Eliza Lynn Linton, 'The Philistine's Coming Triumph', *National Review*, 26 (1895–96), 40–9 (p. 43).

20 Eliza Lynn Linton, 'The Wild Women as Politicians', *Nineteenth Century*, 30 (1891), 79–88 (pp. 82, 79).

21 Sarah Grand, 'Marriage Questions in Fiction', *Fortnightly Review*, n.s. 63 (1898), 378–89 (p. 378); Mona Caird, 'The Morality of Marriage', *Fortnightly Review*, n.s. 47 (1890), 310–30 (p. 330).

22 T. Pilkington White, 'Woman in Politics', *Blackwood's Edinburgh Magazine*, 11 (1897), 342–58 (p. 357).

23 Further details of Regina v. Jackson, or the 'Clitheroe case', can be found in Levine, *Victorian Feminism*, pp. 137, 143, 155.

24 Sally Ledger, *The New Woman: Fiction and Feminism at the* fin de siècle (Manchester, 1997), pp. 21–22.

25 George and Weedon Grossmith, *The Diary of a Nobody* (Harmondsworth, 1965), p. 89.

26 Ella Hepworth Dixon, 'Why Women Are Ceasing to Marry' (1899), quoted in Ledger, *The New Woman*, p. 23.

27 Clement Scott, 'A Doll's House', *Theatre* (1889), quoted in Michael Egan, ed., *Ibsen: The Critical Heritage* (London, 1972), p. 107.

28 Edith Lees, 'Olive Schreiner and her Relation to the Woman Movement' (1915), in Cherry Clayton, ed., *Olive Schreiner* (Johannesburg, 1983), pp. 46–51 (p. 46).

29 Ella Hepworth Dixon, *The Story of a Modern Woman* (London, 1990), p. 213.

30 M.O.W.O. [Mrs Oliphant], 'The Anti-Marriage League', *Blackwood's Edinburgh Magazine*, 159 (1896), 135–49 (p. 144).
31 James Ashcroft Noble, 'The Fiction of Sexuality', *Contemporary Review*, 67 (1895), 490–98 (p. 493).
32 George Egerton, 'A Cross Line', in *Keynotes and Discords* (London, 1983), pp. 1–36 (p. 18).
33 Vernon Lee, 'Deterioration of Soul', *Fortnightly Review*, n.s. 59 (1896), 928–43 (p. 933).
34 Ronald Hyam, *Britain's Imperial Century, 1815–1914* (Basingstoke, 2nd edn, 1993), p. 184.
35 Much of the following information on the South African situation is taken from Hyam, *Britain's Imperial Century*, pp. 240ff.
36 Bernard Porter, *The Lion's Share: A Short History of British Imperialism, 1850–1995* (London, 1996), p. 180.
37 Joseph Conrad, *Youth, Heart of Darkness and The End of the Tether* (London, 1985), p. 45.
38 Edward Said, 'Conrad's *Heart of Darkness* and the Histories of Empire', in Lyn Pykett, ed., *Reading fin de siècle Fictions* (Harlow, 1996), pp. 223–331 (p. 226).
39 Tim Middleton, ' "Unspeakable Rites": Constructions of Subjectivity in *Heart of Darkness* and *American Psycho*', in Tracey Hill, ed., *Decadence and Danger: Writing, History and the fin de siècle* (Bath, 1997), pp. 181–92 (p.186).
40 Thomas Hardy, *Tess of the D'Urbervilles* (London, 1984), p. 121, ch. 13.
41 Thomas Hardy, *Jude the Obscure* (Harmondsworth, 1978), p. 131, pt. 2, ch. 2.
42 Mrs Oliphant, 'The Anti-Marriage League' (1896), quoted in *Thomas Hardy: The Critical Heritage* (London, 1970), pp. 256–62 (pp. 258, 259).
43 Edmund Gosse, review of *Jude the Obscure* (1896), quoted in *Thomas Hardy: The Critical Heritage*, pp. 262–70 (pp. 267, 269).
44 Michael Millgate, *Thomas Hardy: A Biography* (Oxford, 1982), p. 275.
45 D.H. Lawrence, from *Study of Thomas Hardy*, quoted in A.A.H. Inglis, ed., *D.H. Lawrence: A Selection from Phoenix* (Harmondsworth, 1971), p. 249.

Extracts

1   Henry Mayhew, *London Labour and the London Poor* (1849–50)

From 'Of the Children Street-Sellers of London'

Each year sees an increase of the numbers of street-children to a very considerable extent, and the exact nature of their position may be thus briefly depicted: what little *information* they receive is obtained from the worst class – from cheats, vagabonds, and rogues; what little *amusement* they indulge in, springs from sources the most poisonous – the most fatal to happiness and welfare; what little they know of a *home* is necessarily associated with much that is vile and base; their very means of existence, uncertain and precarious as it is, is to a great extent identified with petty chicanery, which is quickly communicated by one to the other; while their physical sufferings from cold, hunger, exposure to the weather, and other causes of a similar nature, are constant, and at times extremely severe. Thus every means by which a proper intelligence may be conveyed to their minds is either closed or at the least tainted, while every duct by which a bad description of knowledge may be infused is sedulously cultivated and enlarged. Parental instruction; the comforts of a home, however humble – the great moral truths upon which society itself rests; – the influence of proper example; the power of education; the effect of useful amusement; are all denied to them, or come to them so greatly vitiated, that they rather tend to increase, than to repress, the very evils they were intended to remedy.

The costers invariably say that no persons under the age of fifteen should be allowed by law to vend articles in the streets; the reason they give for this is – that the children under that period of life having fewer wants and requiring less money to live than those who are older, will sell at a less profit than is fair to expect the articles sold should yield, and thus they tersely conclude, 'they perverts others living, and ruins theirselves'.

There probably is truth in this remark, and I must confess that, for the sake of the children themselves, I should have no objection to see the suggestion acted upon; and yet there immediately rises the plain yet startling question – in such a case, what is to become of the children?

From 'Of Children Sent Out as Street-Sellers by Their Parents'

From one little girl I had the following account. She was then selling boot-laces and offered them most perseveringly. She was turned nine, she said, and had sold things in the streets for two years past, but not regularly. The father got his living in the streets by 'playing', she seemed reluctant to talk about his avocation, but I found that he was sometimes a street-musician, or street-performer, and sometimes sung or recited in public houses, and having 'seen better days', had it appears communicated some feeling of dislike for his present pursuits to his daughter, so that I discontinued any allusion to the subject. The mother earned 2s. or 2s. 6d. weekly, in shoe-binding, when she had employment, which was three weeks out of four, and a son of thirteen earned what was sufficient to maintain him as an (occasional) assistant in a wholesale pottery, or rather pot-shop.

'It's in the winter, sir, when things are far worst with us. Father can make very little then – but I don't know what he earns exactly at any time – and though mother has more work then, there's fire and candle to pay for. We were very badly off last winter, and worse, I think, the winter before. Father sometimes came home and had made nothing, and if mother had no work in hand we went to bed to save fire and candle, if it was ever so soon. Father would die afore he would let mother take as much as a loaf from the parish. I was sent out to sell nuts first: "If it's only 1d. you make," mother said, "it's a good piece of bread." I didn't mind being sent out. I knew children that sold things in the streets. Perhaps I liked it better than staying at home without a fire and with nothing to do, and if I went out I saw other children busy. No, I wasn't a bit frightened when I first started, not a bit. Some children – but they was such little things – said: "O, Liz, I wish I was you." I had twelve ha'porths and sold them all. I don't know what it made; 2d. most likely. I didn't crack a single nut myself. I was fond of them then, but I don't care for them now. I could do better if I went into public-houses, but I'm only let go to Mr Smith's, because he knows father, and Mrs Smith and him recommends me and wouldn't let anybody mislest me. Nobody ever offered to. I hear people swear there sometimes, but it's not at me. I sell nuts to children in the streets, and laces to young women. I have sold nuts and oranges to soldiers. They never say anything rude to me, never. I was once in a great crowd, and was getting crushed, and there was a very tall soldier close by me, and he lifted me, basket and all, right up to his shoulder, and carried me clean out of the crowd. He had stripes on his arm. "I shouldn't like you to be in such a trade," says he, "if you was my child." He didn't say why he wouldn't like it. Perhaps because it was beginning to rain. Yes, we are far better off now. Father makes money. I don't go out in bad weather in the summer; in the winter, though, I must. I don't know what I make. I don't know what I shall be when I grow up. I can read a little. I've been to church five or six times in my life. I should go oftener and so would mother, if we had clothes.'

2   From 'Recapitulation and Conclusion', in Charles Darwin, *The Origin of Species By Means of Natural Selection, or, The Preservation of Favoured Races in the Struggle for Life* (1859)

In the distant future I see open fields for far more important researches. Psychology will be based on a new foundation, that of the necessary acquirement of each mental power and capacity by gradation. Light will be thrown on the origin of man and his history.

Authors of the highest eminence seem to be fully satisfied with the view that each species has been independently created. To my mind it accords better with what we know of the laws expressed on matter by the Creator, that the production and extinction of the past and present inhabitants of the world should have been due to secondary causes, like those determining the birth and death of the individual. When I view all beings not as special creations, but as the lineal descendants of some few beings which lived long before the first bed of the Silurian system was deposited, they seem to me to become ennobled. Judging from the past we may safely infer that not one living species will transmit progeny of any kind to a far distant futurity; for the manner in which all organic beings are grouped, shows that the greater number of species of each genus, and all the species of many genera, have left no descendants, but have become utterly extinct. We can so far take a prophetic glance into futurity as to fortell that it will be the common and widely-spread species, belonging to the larger and dominant groups, which will ultimately prevail and procreate new and dominant species. As all the living forms of life are the lineal descendants of those which lived long before the Silurian epoch, we may feel certain that the ordinary succession by generation has never once been broken, and that no cataclysm has desolated the whole world. Hence we may look with some confidence to a secure future of equally appreciable length. And as natural selection works solely by and for the good of each being, all corporeal and mental endowments will tend to progress towards perfection.

It is interesting to contemplate an entangled bank, clothed with many plants of many kinds, with birds singing on the bushes, with various insects flitting about, and with worms crawling through the damp earth, and to reflect that these elaborately constructed forms, so different from each other, and dependent on each other in so complex a manner, have all been produced by laws acting around us. These laws, taken in the largest sense, being Growth with Reproduction; Inheritance which is almost implied by reproduction, Variability from the indirect and direct action of the external conditions of life, and from use and disuse; a Ratio of Increase so high as to lead to a Struggle for Life, and as a consequence to Natural Selection, entailing Divergence of Character and the Extinction of less-improved forms. Thus, from the war of nature, from famine and death, the most exalted object which we are capable of conceiving, namely, the production of the higher animals, directly follows. There is grandeur in this view of life, with its several powers, having been originally breathed into a few forms or into one; and that, whilst this planet has gone cycling on according to the fixed law of gravity, from so simple a beginning endless forms most beautiful and most wonderful have been, and are being, evolved.

3   From Leslie Stephen, 'The Moral Element in Literature', *Cornhill Magazine*, 43 (1881)

The true service which any great writer renders to his age is not to be summed up by calculating the amount of information, as to facts, or the number of verifiable theories which he has propounded. He is great so far as he has been the mouthpiece through which some new and fruitful idea has been added to the general current of thought. ... Now, it is un-doubtedly a matter of great importance to every one capable of intellectual

interests that he should bring himself into frequent and close contact with
the great men of all times, and especially with the great men of our own
time; for if such men are uttering old truths they are yet bringing out those
aspects, and clothing them in those forms, which are most important at the
present day. Nobody, I need hardly say, can appreciate the great issues of
the time, or sympathise with the great currents of thought, who has not
been more or less at home with the writings of men such as Mr Carlyle, or
Cardinal Newman, or J.S. Mill, or Mr Darwin, or Mr Tennyson, or Mr
Browning – I will mention no one whose name could excite a controversy.
And the service such men render is not that they impress upon us some
specific moral lesson, or that they provide us with additional arguments
against stealing, lying or drunkenness; but that they rouse, excite, and
elevate our whole natures – set us thinking, and therefore enable us to
escape from the fetters of ancient prejudice and worn-out platitudes, or
make us perceive beauty in external nature, or set before us new ideals of
life, of which we should otherwise have been indifferent. But we have to be
co-operative in the result, if it is to be of any real value. We are not to be
buckets to be pumped into, as Mr Carlyle puts it, mere receptacles for
ready-made ideas, but fellow-creatures capable of being roused into
independent activity. Now, in this sense, it is difficult to say where a man
may not find some valuable matter. An active-minded man should be
awake to all the interests of the day, and should find food for thought
everywhere . . . he may even learn something as to the ways of thought and
feeling of his neighbours from novels of the vapid and sentimental, or
purely silly order. . . . I am often half inclined to think that the next best
thing to a good book is a bad book; for, after all, the one hopeless evil is
our stagnation of mind. . . .

To get from literature the best that can be got from it, to use books as
instruments for developing our whole natures, the true secret is to select our
friends; to become as intimate as possible with some of the greatest thinkers
of mankind, and to study works of some great minds until we have been
saturated with their influence, and have assimilated and made part of
ourselves the sentiments which they express most vigorously. To study
literature is not merely (as has been said) to know what has been best said
by the greatest men, but to learn to know those men themselves. In so
doing, the particular moral doctrines which they inculcate, or the effect
upon our moral nature of their teaching, is only a part of the whole
influence. But still it is a part of no small importance, and the condition
upon which a man is able to exert such influence is a profound interest in
those ideas with which purely ethical teaching is strictly bound up; and,
moreover, a capacity for feeling rightly and vigorously upon ethical

questions. In that sense, it is impossible ever really to exclude moral considerations from aesthetical judgements.

4 From H.E. Harvey, 'The Voice of Woman', *Westminster Review*, 145 (1896)

It is only during the last twenty years or so that the voice of woman has really been heard in literature. The women who distinguished themselves as writers before that time wrote under the influence of the social laws and literature which had been established by male feeling – because it was their interest to do so. Being entirely dependent on marriage as a profession, the woman of the past found it her interest to train herself in those qualities which made her attractive to men, humility being conspicuous among them. Even Charlotte Brontë, one of the most original and independent of women writers, stoutly maintained the inferiority of women.

This necessity of meeting the demands of the marriage market has given to the sex an artificial character of subservience and servility which I suppose was pleasing to the men of the past; and is still to a large number; but I observe that for the most part the men of the present day are more ready to admire women of an independent turn of mind.

. . .

Man has always posed as the protector of the weaker sex; but, with the best intentions, is it possible that he can thoroughly understand the interests of a creature different from himself, without consulting her opinion? The law which denied property to married women proved that he did not. Now, the woman of the present day has suddenly discovered that she has opinions of her own respecting her welfare; and those men and women who deride the extravagance of some of the female writers of our times would do well, before they scoff, to consider calmly what these women have to say, and see if there is any cause for their complaints.

. . .

But now those women who dare to make complaint of existing social institutions are told that they wish to overthrow morality and order, and introduce a state of chaos. The question is, Are we living just now in a state of morality and order? Are there no social abuses that need to be rooted up and done away with? Are there no social laws that press unjustly on the hitherto silent part of the community? Now that so many complaints have been made, all these questions ought to be considered. As women have, on the whole, obediently conformed to the character which was required of them for six thousand years or so, I think that now that they have begun to announce publicly that they have opinions of their own, they are due, at the very least, a fair hearing.

1830–1901
Timeline of key events and publications

1830   Accession of William IV
        Revolution in France
        Liverpool to Manchester railway opened
1831   Darwin's voyage on the *Beagle*
        British Society for the Advancement of Science inaugurates annual
        meetings
1832   The Great Reform Act
        Invention of the telegraph
        Cholera epidemic
1833   Beginning of the Oxford Movement
        Factory Act
        Carlyle, *Sartor Resartus*
        Abolition of slavery in British Dominions
1834   Poor Law Amendment Act
        National Gallery founded
1835   Fox Talbot's first photographs
        Municipal Reform Act (England)
        Dickens, *Sketches by Boz*
1836   Railway mania starts
        Dickens, *Pickwick Papers* (–1837)
1837   Accession of Queen Victoria
        Dickens, *Oliver Twist*
        Carlyle, *The French Revolution: A History*
1838   People's Charter proclaimed
        Anti-Corn Law League founded in Manchester
        Dickens, *Nicholas Nickleby* (–1839)

1839   Chartist petition and riots
        Anglo-Chinese opium wars
        Faraday, *Experimental Researches in Electricity*
1840   Victoria and Albert marry
        Penny Post begun
        Dickens, *The Old Curiosity Shop* (–1841)
1841   *Punch* founded
        First census to record women's occupations
        Dickens, *Barnaby Rudge*
1842   Second chartist petition rejected, leading to riots
        Mines Act
        Chadwick, *Sanitary Condition of the Labouring Population of Great Britain*
1843   Annexation of Sind
        Wordsworth becomes Poet Laureate
        Dickens, *A Christmas Carol* and *Martin Chuzzlewit* (–1844)
1844   Factory Act limiting working hours
        Chambers, *Vestiges of the Natural History of Creation*
1845   Newman converted to Roman Catholicism
        Irish famine begins
        Disraeli, *Sybil*
1846   Repeal of the corn laws
        A record 272 railway construction bills enacted
        Dickens, *Dombey and Son* (–1848)
1847   Ten Hours Factory Act
        Communist League founded
        The Brontë sisters publish *Agnes Grey*, *Jane Eyre*, and *Wuthering Heights*
        Thackeray, *Vanity Fair* (–1848)
1848   European revolutions
        Founding of the Pre-Raphaelite Brotherhood
        Collapse of Chartism
        Gaskell, *Mary Barton*
        Mill, *Principle of Political Economy*
        Marx and Engels, *The Communist Manifesto*
1849   Disraeli becomes Conservative leader in the Commons
        C. Brontë, *Shirley*
        Dickens, *David Copperfield* (–1850)
        Mayhew, *London Labour and the London Poor* (–1850)
1850   Tennyson becomes Poet Laureate after Wordsworth's death, and publishes *In Memoriam*

1850   Restoration of the Roman Catholic hierarchy in England and Wales
           Household Words is founded

1851   The Great Exhibition
           Census of religious attendance
           Gaskell, *Cranford*

1852   King's Cross station completed
           Dickens, *Bleak House* (–1853)
           Ford Madox Brown, 'The Last of England'

1853   Compulsory Vaccination Act
           C. Brontë, *Villette*
           Gaskell, *Ruth*

1854   Crimean War (–1856)
           Dickens, *Hard Times*
           Gaskell, *North and South* (–1855)
           Patmore, *The Angel in the House*

1855   Livingstone discovers Victoria Falls
           Dickens, *Little Dorrit* (–1857)
           Trollope, *The Warden*

1856   Annexation of Oudh
           Police Act

1857   Indian Mutiny
           Divorce Act
           Eliot, *Scenes of Clerical Life*
           Founding of Science Museum, Kensington, and National Portrait
           Gallery

1858   Elizabeth Blackwell registered as a doctor

1859   Collins, *The Woman in White* (–1860)
           Eliot, *Adam Bede*
           Dickens, *A Tale of Two Cities*
           Smiles, *Self-Help*
           Mill, *On Liberty*
           Darwin, *On the Origin of Species*
           Mrs Beeton's Book of Household Management (–1861)

1860   Dickens, *Great Expectations* (–1861)
           Eliot, *The Mill on the Floss*
           Ruskin, *Unto This Last*

1861   Post Office Savings Bank founded
           Prince Albert dies
           Abolition of death penalty for sodomy

1862   Discovery of the source of the Nile
           Braddon, *Lady Audley's Secret*

1862   Mill, *Utilitarianism*
1863   Whiteley's department store opens in Bayswater
        Football Association founded
        Work begins on the Albert Memorial
        Gaskell, *Sylvia's Lovers* and 'Cousin Phillis'
1864   First Contagious Diseases Act (also in 1866 and 1869)
        Metropolitan Railway opens
        Gaskell, *Wives and Daughters* (–1866)
1865   Eyre controversy in Jamaica
        Cambridge local exams officially open to women
        Medical college for midwives established
        Ruskin, *Sesame and Lilies*
1866   Women's suffrage petition presented to parliament by J.S. Mill
        Eliot, *Felix Holt*
        Trollope, The Last Chronicle of Barset (–1867)
1867   Second Reform Act
        Antiseptic system for surgery devised
        Marx published first volume of *Das Kapital*
1868   Last public execution, and end of practice of transportation
        First Trades Union Congress
        Collins, *The Moonstone*
1869   Church of Ireland disestablished
        Foundation of Ladies' National Association for Repeal of the
        Contagious Diseases Acts
        Suez Canal opened
1870   Forster's Elementary Education Act
        First Married Women's Property Act
        Civil Service Reforms
        Dickens dies, leaving *Edwin Drood* unfinished
1871   Bank Holidays established
        Stanley and Livingstone meet
        Eliot, *Middlemarch* (–1872)
1872   Girton established as a college
        (Secret) Ballot Act
        Hardy, *Under the Greenwood Tree*, and *A Pair of Blue Eyes*
        (–1873)
1873   Home Rule League established in Ireland
        Anorexia nervosa identified
        Pater, *The Renaissance*
1874   Agricultural labourers' strike
        Hardy, *Far From the Madding Crowd*

1874 Trollope, *The Way We Live Now* (–1875)
1875 Government buys minority interest in Suez
Newnham College established
Women sit surgeons' exams, become clerks in the National Savings
Bank, and Poor Law Guardians for the first time
1876 Victoria is declared Empress of India
The telephone is invented
Eliot, *Daniel Deronda*
1877 The Transvaal is annexed
Founding of the Society for the Protection of Ancient Buildings
Wimbledon tennis championships established
1878 University of London admits women to degrees
Salvation Army founded
Hardy, *The Return of the Native*
1879 Land war in Ireland
Invention of the electric light bulb
1880 Elementary Education made compulsory in England and Wales
Parnell chairs Home Rule party
Death of George Eliot
1881 Gladstone's second Irish Land Act; Parnell arrested, and Land
League proscribed
Natural History Museum founded
Women work as clerks in the Civil Service
1882 Phoenix Park murders
Second Married Women's Property Act
Trams are first seen in London
1883 Contagious Diseases Acts suspended
Stevenson, *Treasure Island*
Schreiner, *The Story of an African Farm*
1884 Fabian Society founded
London convention on the Transvaal meets
Third Reform Act
1885 General Gordon killed
Criminal Law Amendment Act
Dictionary of National Biography founded
Haggard, *King Solomon's Mines*
1886 Trafalgar Square riots
Haggard, *She* (–1887)
Hardy, *The Mayor of Casterbridge* and *The Woodlanders* (–1887)
Stevenson, *The Strange Case of Dr Jekyll and Mr Hyde* and
Kidnapped

1887   Victoria's Golden Jubilee
       Bloody Sunday
       Conan Doyle, *A Study in Scarlet*
1888   Kodak box camera invented
       Jack the Ripper murders in Whitechapel
       First women elected to London County Council
       Kipling, *Plain Tales from the Hills*
1889   First English performance of Ibsen's *A Doll's House*
       International Congress of Psychology in Paris
       Booth, *Life and Labour in London* (–1903)
1890   Cecil Rhodes made premier of the Cape Colony
       Morris, *News from Nowhere*
       Wilde, *The Picture of Dorian Gray*
1891   The Clitheroe case
       Hardy, *Tess of the D'Urbervilles*
       Gissing, *New Grub Street*
1892   G. and W. Grossmith, *The Diary of a Nobody*
       Wilde, *Lady Windermere's Fan*
       Shaw, *Widowers' Houses*
1893   Independent Labour Party founded
       Egerton, *Keynotes*
       Wilde, *A Woman of No Importance*
1894   Women permitted to stand for Parish and District councils
       Yellow Book founded
       Kipling, *The Jungle Book*
       Hardy, *Jude the Obscure* (–1895)
1895   Oscar Wilde is found guilty of committing indecent acts; *The
       Importance of Being Earnest* and *An Ideal Husband* are performed
       in London
       Marconi invents wireless telegraphy
       Lumière brothers invent cinematography
1896   Founding of the *Daily Mail*
       London School of Economics opens
1897   National Union of Women's Suffrage Societies established
       Queen Victoria's Diamond Jubilee
       Stoker, *Dracula*
1898   Gladstone dies
       Hong Kong enlarged when Britain leases Chinese territories
       Vagrancy Act increases penalties for homosexual soliciting
1899   Anglo-Boer War (–1902)
       Seats for Female Shop Assistants Act

1899   Conrad, 'Heart of Darkness'
1900   Conquest of Orange Free State and the Transvaal
         Ruskin and Wilde die
         Freud, *The Interpretation of Dreams*
1901   Queen Victoria dies

Suggestions for further reading

General studies of the Victorian period

Charles Breunig, *The Age of Revolution and Reaction, 1789–1850* (New York, 1977).

Asa Briggs, *Victorian Cities* (London, 1963).

Asa Briggs, *Victorian Things* (London, 1988).

Alec Ellis, *Educating Our Masters: Influences on the Growth of Literacy in Victorian Working-Class Children* (Aldershot, 1985).

Friedrich Engels, *The Condition of the Working Class in England* (Harmondsworth, 1987).

R.C.K. Ensor, *England, 1870–1914* (Oxford, 1936).

Robin Gilmour, *The Intellectual and Cultural Context of English Literature, 1830–1890* (Harlow, 1993).

Jose Harris, *Private Lives, Public Spirit: Britain, 1870–1914* (Harmondsworth, 1994).

K. Theodore Hoppen, *The Mid-Victorian Generation, 1846–1886* (Oxford, 1998).

Peter Jones, *The 1848 Revolutions* (Harlow, 1981).

Howard Martin, *Britain in the Nineteenth Century* (Walton-on-Thames, 1996).

Colin Matthew, ed., *The Nineteenth Century, 1815–1901* (Oxford, 2000).

Lynda Nead, *Victorian Babylon: People, Streets, and Images in Nineteenth-Century London* (New Haven, 2000).

Thomas Richards, *The Commodity Culture of Victorian England: Advertising and Spectacle, 1851–1914* (London, 1991).

Herbert Tucker, ed., *A Companion to Victorian Literature and Culture* (Oxford, 1999).

Raymond Williams, *Culture and Society, 1780–1950* (London, 1958).

Anthony Wood, *Nineteenth-Century Britain, 1815–1914* (Harlow, 2nd edn, 1982).

E.L. Woodward, *The Age of Reform, 1815–1870* (Oxford, 1938).

Novels and readers

Nigel Cross, *The Common Writer: Life in Nineteenth-Century Grub Street* (Cambridge, 1985).

Delia Da Sousa Correa, ed., *The Nineteenth-Century Novel: Realisms* (London, 2000).

Deirdre David, ed., *The Cambridge Companion to the Victorian Novel* (Cambridge, 2001).

Elizabeth Deeds Ermarth, *The English Novel in History, 1840–1895* (London, 1997).

Kate Flint, ed., *The Victorian Novelist: Social Problems and Social Change* (London, 1987).

Kate Flint, *The Woman Reader, 1837–1914* (Oxford, 1993).

Robin Gilmour, *The Idea of the Gentleman in the Victorian Novel* (London, 1981).

Guinevere L. Griest, *Mudie's Circulating Library and the Victorian Novel* (Bloomington, 1970).

Michael Holquist, *Dialogism: Bakhtin and His World* (London, 1990).

John O. Jordan and Robert L. Pattern, eds, *Literature in the Market-Place: Nineteenth-Century British Publishing and Reading Practices* (Cambridge, 1995).

Peter Keating, *The Haunted Study: A Social History of the English Novel, 1875–1914* (London, 1989).

Georg Lukacs, *The Historical Novel*, trans. by Hannah and Stanley Mitchell (London, 1962).

Lyn Pykett, *The Sensation Novel* (London, 1994).

David Trotter, *The English Novel in History, 1895–1920* (London, 1993).

Industry

Rosemarie Bodenheimer, *The Politics of Story in Victorian Social Fiction* (Ithaca, NY, 1988).

M.J. Daunton, *House and Home in the Victorian City: Working-Class Housing, 1850–1914* (London, 1983).

Catherine Gallagher, *The Industrial Reformation of English Fiction, 1832–1867* (Chicago, 1985).

Edward Royle, *Chartism* (Harlow, 1980).

Dorothy and Alan Shelston, *The Industrial City, 1820–1870* (Basingstoke, 1990).

E.P. Thompson, *The Making of the English Working Class* (London, 1966).

Arlene Young, *Culture, Class and Gender in the Victorian Novel: Gentlemen, Gents and Working Women* (Basingstoke, 1999).

Religion

Owen Chadwick, *The Victorian Church* (2 vols, Oxford, 1966, 1970).

Valentine Cunningham, *Everywhere Spoken Against: Dissent in the Victorian Novel* (Oxford, 1975).

Hilary Fraser, *Beauty and Belief: Aesthetics and Religion in Victorian Literature* (Cambridge, 1986).

Elisabeth Jay, *The Religion of the Heart: Anglican Evangelicalism and the Nineteenth-Century Novel* (Oxford, 1979).

Elisabeth Jay, *Faith and Doubt in Victorian Britain* (Basingstoke, 1986).

John Maynard, *Victorian Discourses on Sexuality and Religion* (Cambridge, 1993).

James R. Moore, ed., *Religion in Victorian Britain* (3 vols, Manchester, 1995).

Gerald Parsons, ed., *Religion in Victorian Britain* (5 vols, Manchester, 1988–97).

Michael Wheeler, *Heaven, Hell and the Victorians* (Cambridge, 1994).

John Wolffe, *Great Deaths: Grieving, Religion and Nationhood in Victorian and Edwardian Britain* (Oxford, 2000).

Empire

Patrick Brantlinger, *Rule of Darkness: British Literature and Imperialism, 1830–1914* (Ithaca and London, 1988).

Terry Eagleton, *Heathcliff and the Great Hunger* (1995).

Ronald Hyam, *Britain's Imperial Century, 1815–1914* (Basingstoke, 2nd edn, 1993).

Suvendrini Perera, *Reaches of Empire: The English Novel from Edgeworth to Dickens* (New York, 1991).

Bernard Porter, *The Lion's Share: A Short History of British Imperialism, 1850–1995* (London, 1996).

Edward Said, *Culture and Imperialism* (New York, 1993).

Women and sexuality

Michel Foucault, *The History of Sexuality: An Introduction* (Harmondsworth, 1978).

Elizabeth K. Helsinger, Robin Lauterbach Sheets and William Veeder, eds, *The Woman Question: Society and Literature in Britain and America, 1837–1883, volume 2: Social Issues* (Chicago, 1983).

Philippa Levine, *Victorian Feminism, 1850–1900* (London, 1987).

Michael Mason, *The Making of Victorian Sexuality* (Oxford, 1994).

Michael Mason, *The Making of Victorian Sexual Attitudes* (Oxford, 1994).

Deborah Epstein Nord, *Walking the Victorian Streets: Women, Representation and the City* (Ithaca and London, 1995).

Mary Poovey, *Uneven Developments: The Ideological Work of Gender in Mid-Victorian England* (Chicago, 1988).

Eve Kosofsky Sedgwick, *Between Men: English Literature and Male Homosocial Desire* (New York, 1985).

Mary Lyndon Shanley, *Feminism, Marriage and the Law in Victorian England, 1850–1895* (Princeton, 1989).

Judith R. Walkowitz, *City of Dreadful Delight: Narratives of Sexual Danger in Late-Victorian London* (Chicago, 1992).

Jeffrey Weeks, *Sex, Politics and Society: The Regulation of Sexuality since 1800* (London and New York, 1981).

Science

Gillian Beer, *Darwin's Plots: Evolutionary Narrative in Darwin, George Eliot and Nineteenth-Century Fiction* (London, 1985).

George Levine, *Darwin and the Novelists: Patterns of Science in Victorian Fiction* (Cambridge, MA, 1988).

Bernard Lightman, *Victorian Science in Context* (Chicago, 1997).

Roy M. MacLeod, *The 'Creed of Science' in Victorian England* (Aldershot, 2000).

Sally Shuttleworth, *George Eliot and Nineteenth-Century Science* (Cambridge, 1984).

Helen Small, *Love's Madness: Medicine, the Novel, and Female Insanity, 1800–1865* (Oxford, 1996).

Jenny Bourne Taylor and Sally Shuttleworth, eds, *Embodied Selves: An Anthology of Psychological Texts, 1830–1890* (Oxford, 1998).

Jane Wood, *Passion and Pathology in Victorian Fiction* (Oxford, 2000).

Fin de siècle

Stephen Arata, *Fictions of Loss in the Victorian Fin de Siècle* (Cambridge, 1996).

Ann Ardis, *New Women, New Novels: Feminism and Early Modernism* (New Brunswick, 1990).

Ian Fletcher, ed., *Decadence and the 1890s* (London, 1979).

Holbrook Jackson, *The Eighteen Nineties* (London, 1913).

Sally Ledger, *The New Woman* (Manchester, 1997).

Sally Ledger and Scott McCracken, eds, *Cultural Politics at the Fin de Siècle* (Cambridge, 1995).

Elaine Showalter, *Sexual Anarchy: Gender and Culture at the* fin de siècle (London, 1990).

John Stokes, *In the Nineties* (Hemel Hempstead, 1989).

The visual arts

Tim Barringer, *The Pre-Raphaelites* (London, 1998).

Dianne Sachko Macleod, *Art and the Victorian Middle-Class: Money and the Making of Cultural Identity* (Cambridge, 1996).

Elizabeth Prettejohn, ed., *After the Pre-Raphaelites: Art and Aestheticism in Victorian England* (Manchester, 1999).

Alison Smith, *The Victorian Nude: Sexuality, Morality and Art* (Manchester, 1996).

Hugh Witemeyer, *George Eliot and the Visual Arts* (New Haven and London, 1979).

Christopher Wood, *Olympian Dreamers: Victorian Classical Painters, 1860–1914* (London, 1983).

Christopher Wood, *Victorian Painters* (Woodbridge, 1995).

Theatre

Michael Booth, *Theatre in the Victorian Age* (Cambridge, 1991).

Anthony Jenkins, *The Making of Victorian Drama* (Cambridge, 1991).

Joseph Litvak, *Caught in the Act: Theatricality in the Nineteenth-Century English Novel* (Berkeley, 1992).

Gail Marshall, *Actresses on the Victorian Stage* (Cambridge, 1998).

Kerry Powell, *Women and Victorian Theatre* (Cambridge, 1997).

George Rowell, *The Victorian Theatre, 1792–1914* (Cambridge, 1978).

John Russell Stephens, *The Profession of the Playwright: British Theatre, 1800–1900* (Cambridge, 1992).

George Taylor, *Players and Performances in the Victorian Theatre* (Manchester, 1989).

Index